AKE IT MINNESOTAN !

Sesquicentennial Cookbook

*50 Years of Recipes and Stories
from Minnesota Kitchens*

MAKE IT MINNESOTAN!
Sesquicentennial Cookbook

150 Years of Recipes and Stories
from Minnesota Kitchens

The Minnesota
Sesquicentennial
Cookbook Committee

Claire Plank, project manager

Anne Lauer, chairperson

MaryJo Boyle   Deborah Kreger
Pat Edlund   Donna Jo Schiltz
Sally Fashant   Chris Sturzl
Sharon Haley   Carol Taggart

edited by Patricia Miller

foreword by Sue Zelickson

NODIN PRESS

Cover photos, clockwise from upper left—pie crust, Tamara
Cordeschi; corn, Arlene Gardinier; women in kitchen, Arlene
Gardinier; bake-off winners: Maja Sahlberg.
Back cover photo and chapter photos: John Toren
Design and layout: John Toren
Printed at Bang Printing: Brainerd, Minnesota

Second Printing

Library of Congress Cataloging-in-Publication Data

Make it Minnesotan! : sesquicentennial cookbook : 150 years
recipes and stories from Minnesota kitchens / prepared by t
Minnesota Sesquicentennial Cookbook Committee ; Claire Pla
chairperson ; edited by Patricia Miller.
      p. cm.
   Includes index.
   ISBN 978-1-932472-74-5
   1. Cookery, American. 2. Cookery--Minnesota. 3. Cooke
International. I. Miller, Patricia. II. Minnesota Sesquicentenn
Commission.
   TX715.M24853 2008
   641.59776--dc22
                                          2008022982

Nodin Press, LLC
530 North Third Street,
Suite 120,
Minneapolis, MN 55401

This book is dedicated to the cooks throughout Minnesota who generously contributed the recipes, both traditional and innovative, and shared the stories behind them.

IN HONOR OF MINNESOTA'S SESQUICENTENNIAL, we have endeavo
to create a cookbook that captures the cultural traditions and culi
specialties that make the state's cooking unique, while also reflecting
ways that Minnesotans come together around food in the 21ˢᵗ century. A
countless hours of sifting through recipes for lefse, klub, potica and sʋ
cookies—and heated discussions on more than one occasion—we hɑ
cookbook. Actually, we had more than a cookbook. We had a snapshɔ
Minnesota at its 150ᵗʰ anniversary. We had recipes sprinkled with stc
and stories highlighted by their recipes. We found that Minnesotans
great storytellers, but even better cooks!

Make it Minnesotan would never have been possible without
generous support of Nodin Press. The enthusiasm of Norton Stillr
and John Toren in the design and production of the book was gre
appreciated. Our editor, Patricia Miller, deserves special kudos.
creative suggestions and, above all, patience, helped steer the direc
of this book.

A hearty "Thank You!" goes to the hard-working members of
Minnesota Sesquicentennial Cookbook Committee, who not only r
through the recipes but tested them, differentiating the outstanɔ
entries from the good and merely "interesting" ones. They also shɔ
dered the more mundane task of converting numerous "T's" into "tal
spoons"—a feat for only the true chef.

And of course, many thanks to the hundreds of Minnesota co
who took the time to share their recipes and stories. What fun we
sampling your creations!

The following pages offer a fascinating peek into kitchens throu
out the state. Enjoy the stories … and enjoy the food!

Claire Pla
Minnesota Sesquicentennial Cookbook project manaɡ

May 11, 2ɔ

Table of Contents

Foreword by Sue Zelickson .... *ix*

Northwest 1

Recipes from Becker, Big Stone, Clay, Clearwater, Douglas, Grant, Kittson, Mahnomen, Marshall, Norman, Otter Tail, Pennington, Polk, Pope, Red Lake, Roseau, Stevens, Traverse and Wilkin counties

Northeast 41

Recipes from Aitkin, Beltrami, Carlton, Cass, Cook, Crow Wing, Hubbard, Itasca, Kanabec, Koochiching, Lake, Lake of the Woods, Mille Lacs, Morrison, Pine, St. Louis, Todd and Wadena counties

Central 81

Recipes from Anoka, Benton, Carver, Chisago, Hennepin, Isanti, McLeod, Meeker, Ramsey, Sherburne, Stearns, Washington and Wright counties

Southeast 127

Recipes from Blue Earth, Dakota, Dodge, Faribault, Fillmore, Freeborn, Goodhue, Houston, Le Sueur, Mower, Olmsted, Rice, Scott, Steele, Wabasha, Waseca and Winona counties

Southwest 169

Recipes from Brown, Chippewa, Cottonwood, Jackson, Kandiyohi, Lac Qui Parle, Lincoln, Lyon, Martin, Murray, Nicollet, Nobles, Pipestone, Redwood, Renville, Rock, Sibley, Swift, Watonwan and Yellow Medicine counties

Index 214

Index of Contributors 221

The 17-member Minnesota Statehood Sesquicentennia Commission created by the State Legislature in 2005 an appointed in 2006, guided the Sesquicentennial event throughout 2008. Eight members were state legislators Nine members were from across Minnesota and appointed by the Governor. The Commission oversaw several events commemorations and initiatives of statewide significance It also encouraged citizen engagement and grassroots ac tion by local citizens and organizations to create statehood events and projects in all of Minnesota's 87 counties.

Minnesota Sesquicentennial Commission Members: Cay Shea Hellervik, Chair, Reatha Clark King, Vice Chair, Sena tor Don Betzold, Rep. Sondra Erickson, Beth Hartwig, Tess Hohman, Sarah Janecek, Rep. Morrie Lanning, Cal Larson Rep. Diane Loeffler, Senator Pat Pariseau, Mark Peterson Senator Gen Olson, Senator Ann Rest, Dallas Ross, Rep Loren Solberg, Joe C. Swedberg, and Executive Director Jane Leonard

Foreword:
One Hundred Fifty Years of Cooking in Minnesota

How exciting it is to commemorate the Sesquicentennial with this beautiful cookbook filled with foods that were grown and harvested locally, and hand-me-down recipes shared by families from throughout Minnesota.

Many of the recipes have been passed down from generation to generation and each region has specialties and favorites that reflect the cultural and ethnic origins of the people who settled there.

As you draw upon the recipes in this book, it may rekindle the memory of meals from your grandparents' kitchens that you loved as a child, and it will surely be the source of some new eating traditions in your own family.

Among the recipes from central Minnesota you will find Swedish pancakes, oyster stew, German potato salad, and sauerkraut from scratch. The Northeast section brings us wild rice breads and soup recipes, Iron Miner pasties, pirogues, venison meatballs, and blueberry coffee cake. The Northwest highlights include klub, lefse, rosettes, and rhubarb recipes for slush, crunch, breads and more. In the Southeast region the cooks love to bake so they shared recipes for English muffins, potica, and Hazel's $10,000 Cheesecake, which I can't wait to try.

Now if your ancestors came from Southwestern Minnesota, you will love learning (or being reminded) how to make abbleskiver, hoppel poppel, and Indian fry bread, as well as many jams and pies.

No matter where you hail from or where you live now, if you spend time in Minnesota you'll have the opportunity to sample tasty hotdishes and casseroles, and there are plenty of these recipes from every region to explore here.

Make It Minnesotan! will help us recall the state's distinguished past, celebrate our present, and provide a link with future generations through cooking, eating, and fondly reflecting on the blessings of living in the marvelous state of Minnesota.

Sue Zelickson

– Sue Zelickson
food editor, WCCO radio

NORTHWEST REGION

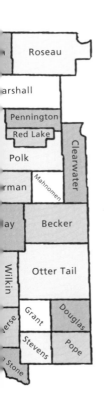

In Minnesota's "big-sky" country of the Northwest, follow the Klub Route and discover a potato-dumpling delicacy claimed by both Germans and Scandinavians. Or pull up a chair at a church supper and dig into a big wedge of rhubarb custard pie with a cup of puts-hair-on-your-chest coffee, of course. Or try to decide which oh-so-good bars or cookies you'll take home from the school bake sale. In this region where the prairies meet the pines, you'll find foods just like Mom and Dad still make!

Rhubarb Slush

Anne Hanson ◆ Traverse County

Try this cool, summery punch made with rhubarb fresh from the garden.

> 2 quarts rhubarb, cut into 1-inch pieces
> 2 quarts water
> 1 (3-ounce) package strawberry gelatin
> 3 cups sugar
> ½ cup lemon juice

Cook rhubarb with water in an enamel kettle on range or in a microwave dish. Strain liquid through colander or strainer. Discard soft pulp. Add strawberry gelatin, sugar and lemon juice to the hot liquid. Freeze in plastic freezer containers.

For cool beverage mix 2 cups slush with 2 cups ginger ale or other carbonated beverage. Be sure to take slush mix from freezer a couple of hours before putting the punch together.

Yield: 12 to 16 servings

Fruit Salsa and Cinnamon Chips

Karen Gonsorowski ◆ Marshall County

Cinnamon Chips:
½ cup sugar
½ teaspoon cinnamon
10 flour tortillas

Fruit Salsa:
2 kiwis, peeled and chopped
2 apples, peeled and chopped
1 cup strawberries, chopped
juice from 1 orange

Cinnamon Chips: Mix cinnamon and sugar together. Rinse tortillas in water, sprinkle with cinnamon/sugar mixture. Cut into triangles and bake for 8 minutes at 400°. Cool and store in airtight container.

Fruit Salsa: Mix salsa ingredients together gently. Serve with chips.

Yield: 30 chips and 1½ cups salsa

Cheesy Wild Rice Nibblers

Helene Pettil ◆ Otter Tail County

12 slices bread, crusts removed, each slice cut into 3 strips
3 tablespoons butter, softened
½ cup cooked wild rice
½ cup fresh mushrooms, finely chopped
¼ cup green pepper, finely chopped
⅓ cup onion, finely chopped
½ cup Cheddar cheese, grated
¼ cup mayonnaise
½ teaspoon Worcestershire sauce

Spread bread strips with soft butter. Combine rice with remaining ingredients. Broil buttered bread until lightly toasted. Quickly spread with the wild rice mixture and continue to broil until heated through and bubbly.

Yield: 36 appetizers

Fat Rascals (Potato Cheese Puffs)

Brian Halverson ◆ Clay County

I've grown potatoes in the Red River Valley for 50 years, and they get top billing in this fun appetizer recipe.

1 cup mashed potatoes
2 eggs, beaten
½ cup milk
2 cups American or Cheddar
    cheese, shredded

½ cup flour
¼ teaspoon baking powder
salt and pepper to taste
salad oil
sour cream, for serving

Combine all ingredients except oil and sour cream; mix well. Pour about 2 inches of salad oil into a frying pan and heat to 375°. Drop batter by tablespoons, 4 or 5 at a time, into hot oil. Fry 3 to 4 minutes or until golden brown. Serve immediately with sour cream.

Yield: 24 puffs

Bran Muffins

Old Mill State Park ◆ Marshall County

This recipe is from Old Mill State Park and the volunteers who help take care of it. It uses the bran from the stone-ground wheat flour that is milled there every summer.

1 quart buttermilk	4 eggs
5 teaspoons baking soda	5 cups flour
1 cup shortening	5 cups bran
1 teaspoon salt	½ cup nuts, chopped, optional
2 cups sugar	½ cup raisins, optional

Mix buttermilk and soda. Stir until soda dissolves. Set aside. Combine shortening, salt and sugar. Add eggs. Add flour alternately with buttermilk/soda mixture. Mix in the wheat flour. Bake 20 to 25 minutes in a preheated oven at 375º in greased tins. May add nuts and raisins (desired amounts) just before baking.

Yield: 36 to 48 muffins

Cook's Note: This batter will keep in the fridge for several weeks. Keep tightly covered.

Swedish Toast

Twyla Hinneberg ◆ Big Stone County

½ cup butter
1 cup margarine
2 cups sugar
2 eggs
1 cup cultured sour cream
2 teaspoons almond extract
3½ cups flour
⅛ teaspoon salt
2 teaspoons baking powder
1 cup almonds, chopped or sliced

Cream together butter, margarine and sugar. Add the eggs, sour cream and almond extract. Blend in flour, salt, baking powder and almonds. Bake these in 4 small tins about 3x7-inches in size at 350° for 35 to 40 minutes. Cool loaves and let them sit overnight. Then slice thin with an electric knife. Toast these on a cookie sheet at 300°, 10 minutes on each side. Store them in a tightly closed tin, but do not freeze.

Lefse

Muriel Geroy ◆ Roseau County

Lefse is a popular Scandinavian treat in northern Minnesota. It's often served with lutefisk, mashed potatoes, meatballs, or other Scandinavian foods at Thanksgiving or Christmas. It's also popular at church dinners in the fall.

> 6 cups potatoes, boiled and riced
> ½ cup butter
> ⅓ cup half-and-half
> ½ teaspoon salt
> 2 teaspoons sugar
> 1 ½ cups flour

Mix and divide into approximately 12 pieces. Roll out thin, adding more flour if needed. Fry on griddle at 450° to 500° turning to brown both sides.

Yield: Approximately 25 servings

Cook's Note: It's best if you roll the lefse thin and don't add too much flour because this can make it tough. You may cut pieces in half before serving. Spread lefse with butter and sprinkle with sugar.

Pumpkin Pecan Loaves

Carol Seeger ◆ Red Lake County

Bread:
3⅓ cups flour
3 cups sugar
2 teaspoons baking soda
1½ teaspoons salt
1 teaspoon ground cinnamon
1 teaspoon nutmeg
1 (15-ounce) can pumpkin
1 cup vegetable or canola oil
4 eggs, slightly beaten
⅔ cup water
½ cup pecans, chopped

Caramel Glaze:
¼ cup butter or margarine
¼ cup sugar
¼ cup brown sugar, packed
¼ cup whipping cream
⅔ cup confectioner's sugar
1 teaspoon vanilla extract

Bread: Combine flour, sugar, baking soda, salt, cinnamon and nutmeg; set aside. Combine pumpkin, oil, eggs and water; mix well. Stir into dry ingredients until combined. Fold in pecans. Spoon into 2 greased 9x5x3-inch loaf pans.

Bake in a preheated oven at 350° for 60 to 65 minutes. Insert toothpick in center to check for doneness, toothpick should come out clean. Cool for 10 minutes before removing from pans to wire racks.

Caramel Glaze: Combine butter, sugars and whipping cream in sauce pan. Cook until sugar is dissolved. Cool for 20 minutes. Stir in confectioner's sugar and vanilla until smooth. Drizzle over cooled loaves.

Yield: 2 loaves

Maple Pecan French Toast

Suzanne Tweten—The Log House Homestead on Spirit Lake ◆
Otter Tail County

Our Maple Pecan French Toast, served with wild rice sausage, is one of our favorite entrées. We tap our own maple syrup from 60 acres of maple woods that are part of our 115 acres of lakeshore property. We organically grow our own herbs and always bake our own bread. This is a fast and simple recipe that's guaranteed to produce the same delicious breakfast every time.

pecans for top and bottom, chopped or whole
8 challah bread slices

Batter:
8 eggs
¾ cup half-and-half
½ cup sugar
1 teaspoon vanilla
pinch salt

Filling:
1 (8-ounce) package cream cheese, softened
¼ teaspoon vanilla
1 tablespoon orange juice, fresh squeezed
¼ cup pure maple syrup

In the bottom of an 8-inch glass baking pan, spread a layer of pecans. Mix batter ingredients together and soak bread slices in batter for 15 minutes. Discard batter after soaking bread. Lay down 4 slices of wet bread. Spread filling on top of bread. Top with the remaining slices of wet bread. Layer with pecans.

Bake in a preheated oven at 350° for 30 minutes. Serve with hot maple syrup.

Yield: 8 servings

Rhubarb Sunflower Bread

Sonne Labs—Project Breckenridge ◆ Wilkin County

Sunflowers are a common crop in Wilkin County and the Red River Valley, and rhubarb grows in just about everyone's backyard in this part of the state.

Bread:
 1½ cups brown sugar, packed
 ⅔ cup sunflower oil
 1 egg
 1 cup sour milk
 1 teaspoon salt *
 1 teaspoon baking soda
 1 teaspoon vanilla
 2½ cups flour
 1½ cups fresh rhubarb, diced
 ½ cup roasted sunflower kernels

Topping:
 ½ cup sugar
 2 tablespoons butter, softened
 ¼ cup sunflower kernels

Bread: Stir all ingredients together in order given. Put into 2 well-greased loaf pans.

Topping: Mix topping ingredients and sprinkle over both pans of batter. Bake in a preheated oven at 350° for 50 minutes.

Yield: 2 loaves

*Omit salt if using salted sunflower kernels.

Hard Time Soup

Faye Auchenpaugh ◆ Pennington County

According to the 2000 U.S. Census, Thief River Falls is the most Norwegian town in the United States. All four of my grandparents were born in Norway. This recipe was handed down through the family, but its exact origins are unknown. Although the name suggests that the recipe was developed for hard times when there was no meat available, it continues to be our family's favorite seasonal soup. The soup is a complete meal, and we usually serve it for lunch.

The richness of the soil in our area produces great quantities of fresh vegetables of high quality. Hard Time Soup tastes the very best when all of the ingredients have been freshly picked. The fresh vegetables are available at the same time strawberries are producing in the garden. Our dessert is a slice of buttered home-baked bread slathered with strawberries mashed with sugar.

5 medium new potatoes, peeled and cut into 1-inch chunks
8 medium carrots, peeled and sliced
½ medium onion, diced
½ medium-sized cabbage, cut into bite-sized pieces
1 teaspoon salt
½ teaspoon pepper
water
2 cups peas
1 quart half-and-half
whole milk if more liquid is desired, optional
1 tablespoon butter, optional

Put potatoes, carrots and onion in a 4-quart cooking pot, place cabbage on top. Sprinkle with salt and pepper. Add just enough water to barely cover the vegetables. Cook on medium heat until vegetables are tender. Do not drain. Add peas. Pour in cream, stirring constantly, until liquid becomes the consistency of whole milk. Simmer (do not boil) until peas are cooked. Whole milk may be added if more liquid is desired. A tablespoon of butter may also be added for flavor.

Yield: 8 servings

Fish Tacos

Pelican Rapids High School Students ◆ Otter Tail County

I am a Family and Consumer Science teacher at Pelican Rapids High School. Our school is very diverse, considering we are located in rural Minnesota. We have Hispanics, Vietnamese, Bosnians, Somalians and more. I also teach an International Foods class, and the students from these countries share their unique recipes from their home country. The class creates a cookbook each semester that includes all the recipes we have tried during the 18 weeks of the class. The following three recipes are a sample of what we're eating and enjoying in Pelican Rapids.

– Coleen Guhl

Creamy Sauce:
>   1 cup sour cream or use ½ cup sour cream and ½ cup mayo
>   for some zing
>   1 tablespoon lemon juice
>   ½ teaspoon onion powder
>   ½ teaspoon chili powder
>   2 tablespoons taco seasoning

Salsa:
>   3 to 4 medium tomatoes
>   1 fresh jalapeño pepper
>   3 cloves garlic
>   1 small white onion
>   ¼ to ½ bunch cilantro
>   kosher salt to taste

Fish:
>   ½ cup cornmeal
>   ½ teaspoon salt
>   1 tablespoon chili powder
>   1 pound white fish filets, cut into 1-inch strips
>   (white fish could be bass, cod, etc.)

Tacos:
>   ½ head (about 4 cups) green cabbage, finely shredded
>   2 tomatoes, diced
>   8 (6-inch) soft flour tortillas
>   2 limes, quartered

Salsa: Place items in a food processor and process until chunky. Chill.

Creamy Sauce: Mix ingredients together and set aside.

Fish: Stir together the cornmeal, salt and chili powder. Coat the fish strips in the corn meal mixture until coated. Spray the bottom of a shallow baking dish with cooking spray. Place fish strips in baking dish pan. Bake for 10 minutes at 350° or until fish flakes apart.

Tacos: Place tortilla in palm of hand, spoon 1 tablespoon of the cream sauce onto the tortilla and spread out. Place fresh salsa over cream sauce. Place about ¼ cup shredded cabbage onto the tortilla. Top with two or more strips of cooked fish. Drizzle with more sauce, if desired, and top with diced tomatoes. Squeeze lime juice onto the taco and enjoy.

Yield: 8 tacos

Somalian Tea

Pelican Rapids High School Students ◆ Otter Tail County

We all loved this tea!

> 2½ cups sugar
> tea bags
> 1 tablespoon cinnamon, freshly ground
> ½ tablespoons cloves, freshly ground
> 1 tablespoon cardamom, freshly ground

Heat water up a large 12 cup tea kettle. Add 6 tea bags to seep along with the spices. At this point you can put it in a large coffee dispenser to keep hot.

Cook's Note: Some people add about 1½ cups of powdered milk to the tea mixture. Others might add milk to the tea at the time it is put in the tea cup. Others prefer it without the milk.

Mexican Cabbage Salad

Pelican Rapids High School Students ◆ Otter Tail County

1 medium head of cabbage, sliced thin
¼ of a small onion, sliced thin
4 serrano peppers, diced (remove some of the seeds
   if you don't want it too hot!)
4 small tomatoes, diced
1 bunch of cilantro, chopped
juice from 3 limes
1 small bottle of salsa picante
cocktail shrimp, optional
saltine crackers

Mix cabbage and onion. Add serrano peppers, tomatoes and ¾ of the cilantro. Juice 3 limes and sprinkle juice over mixture. Put a heaping serving of cabbage mixture onto saltine crackers or other crackers. Sprinkle salsa picante on top.

Yield: 24 to 30 squares

Cook's Note: You can also add whole cocktail shrimp to this salad to make it a little different.

Wild Rice Soup

Country Belles—Extension Home Study Group ◆ Stevens County

⅓ cup wild rice, uncooked
2 tablespoons butter
1 tablespoon onion, minced
¼ cup flour
4 cups chicken broth
½ teaspoon salt

⅓ cup carrots, shredded
⅓ cup celery, diced
⅓ cup fresh mushrooms,
   sliced
1 cup half-and-half
fresh parsley

Rinse wild rice, soak in cold water 1 hour: drain. Cover with boiling water and cook over low heat for 40 minutes. Melt butter in 4-quart pan and sauté onion. Blend in flour; gradually add broth and cook, stirring until thickened. Stir in rice, salt, carrots, celery and mushrooms. Simmer 5 minutes, add half-and-half. Heat to serve. Garnish with parsley.

Yield: 6 servings

Creamy Ham and Asparagus Soup
Hancock Homemakers—Extension Home Study Group ♦ Stevens County

A delicious spring soup using fresh asparagus and leftover ham.

1 medium carrot, julienned
3 small onions, quartered
2 tablespoons butter
2 tablespoons flour
1 cup milk
1 cup chicken broth
1 cup ham, cubed
1 jar mushrooms, sliced
1 ½ cups fresh asparagus pieces
1 cup half-and-half
salt and pepper, to taste
Parmesan cheese and parsley, optional

Place asparagus in water and cook until tender; drain. Cook carrots and onion in butter until tender. Stir in flour and gradually add milk. Bring to a boil and stir for 2 minutes. Add broth, ham, mushrooms and asparagus. Reduce heat. Add cream and heat, but do not boil. Add salt and pepper. Garnish with Parmesan cheese and parsley if desired.

Yield: 4 to 6 servings

Barbecued Meatballs

Joyce Glad ◆ Kittson County

These meatballs make a traditional meat-and-potatoes meal for your family or gatherings.

Meat Mixture:
    2 pounds ground beef
    ½ cup milk
    ½ cup dry bread crumbs or soda crackers
    2 teaspoons salt
    onion (to taste), chopped

Sauce:
    1 cup brown sugar, packed
    ½ cup ketchup
    2 tablespoons onion, minced
    2 teaspoons prepared mustard

Meat: Mix and shape meat mixture into 2-inch balls. Place meatballs in uncovered pan.

Sauce: Mix sauce ingredients together. Pour over meatballs. Bake at 350° for 45 to 60 minutes.

Yield: 10 to 12 servings

Cook's Notes: Serve with cheesy potatoes or a baked potato and green beans.

No-Crust Vegetarian Quiche

Pat Corbid ◆ Becker County

At the Lady Slipper Inn Bed & Breakfast, we serve this quiche for breakfast. The morning begins with fresh muffins or scones and coffee and tea set out on a buffet for our guests to enjoy before their scheduled breakfast. Once they're seated, we start the meal with a fruit plate followed by our quiche served with toast or toasted English muffins.

8 eggs
1½ cups cottage cheese
1½ cups Cheddar cheese, shredded (reserve ½ cup)
pinch of red pepper and seasoned salt (or use some
    pepper cheese with the Cheddar cheese)
⅓ cup flour
1 teaspoon baking powder
1 cup broccoli, grated
1 cup cauliflower, grated

Preheat oven to 350°. Put eggs, cottage cheese, 1 cup of Cheddar cheese and the dry ingredients in a blender and blend at high for 2 minutes. Spray 9½-inch pie dish with cooking spray. Spread grated broccoli and cauliflower in pie dish. Pour blended egg mixture over vegetables. Spread reserved cheese over the top. Bake 40 to 45 minutes. Let "rest" for at least 5 minutes before cutting to serve.

Yield: 4 to 6 servings

Cook's Notes: Because ovens vary greatly, set the timer for 30 minutes and check every 5 minutes after that. This can sit out of the oven for 15 to 20 minutes very comfortably before serving. Cover to keep warm.

French Meat Pie (Tourtière)

Carol Seeger ◆ Red Lake County

This recipe has been served by the French people in northern Minnesota for holidays as far back as anyone can remember. The method and ingredients have never changed over the years.

1½ pounds lean ground pork
1 onion, chopped
2 potatoes, cooked and mashed
3 slices bread, toasted and diced
salt and pepper to taste
½ teaspoon ground cloves
½ teaspoon cinnamon
½ teaspoon allspice
homemade double crust pastry, unbaked
    or purchased crust

In a skillet, sauté pork and onions on low. Add remaining ingredients and mix. Line pie plate with 1 crust, add filling. Top with remaining crust and flute edges. Bake in a preheated oven at 375° for 30 to 35 minutes until golden brown. Cover edges of crust with aluminum foil if they seem too brown.

Yield: 8 slices

Cook's Note: This pie tastes delicious in a homemade pie crust, but a purchased fold-out crust will do just fine.

Potato Klub (Potato Dumplings)

Ethel Thorlacius ◆ Marshall County

Northwestern Minnesota has a unique eating experience. It's possible to find that Scandinavian favorite—potato klub (pronounced "kloob")—at several country cafes along the highways in the area. These cafes schedule their menus so that Klub is available to eager patrons on several days of the week, and they travel from place to place eating it. It's nicknamed the Klub Route.

Klub is an unusual dish. It probably was a poor man's food, made when times were lean and only basic ingredients were to be had. Perhaps nostalgia has something to do with its popularity. It's a true "comfort" food.

> 1 ham shank
> 4 potatoes, uncooked
> 2 potatoes, boiled
> 1 cup whole wheat flour
> 1 cup white flour
> ¼ teaspoon baking powder
> salt and pepper to taste

Boil the ham shank until done (when meat is loose on bone). Remove it from the liquid and let it cool. Save the liquid. Remove the meat and some of the fat from the bone and put it through a grinder with the potatoes. Add the flours, baking powder, salt and pepper. Be sure there is enough flour to make a stiff dough. Using your hands, roll dough into dumplings, drop into the ham liquid and cook at a slow boil until done (about 1 hour.) Serve the dumplings with butter on top.

Yield: 4 to 6 servings

Overnight Wild Rice

Lois Schaedler ◆ Mahnomen County

Wild rice takes between 45 minutes and one hour to cook. This recipe allows you to put it in the oven when you go to bed and awake to cooked wild rice. Very easy!

    wild rice
    water, boiling

Use four times the water as to the rice, or follow directions on wild rice package (example: 1 cup rice to 4 cups water).

Preheat oven to 450°. Rinse rice well 3 times. In a large oven-proof dish place rice and water allowing room for rice to swell. Stir. Turn oven off. Place dish into oven, in the morning rice will be cooked.

Cook's Note: Use cooked wild rice in stuffings, as a side dish, in tuna or chicken salad or as a hot breakfast cereal.

Ziggy Burgers

Norman A. Shelsta ◆ Big Stone County

This recipe originated at Sigloh's Café, which was in business during the 1950s and '60s in Ortonville. Recently, various groups have used it at fundraisers and other social gatherings.

    5 pounds lean ground beef, browned
    ½ can tomato soup
    2 cups tomato juice
    1 teaspoon black pepper
    4 teaspoons salt
    4 teaspoons chili powder
    4 heaping teaspoons brown sugar
    4 teaspoons powdered mustard
    1 large onion, diced
    sliced buns

Put all ingredients together in a pan and cook over medium heat until done; stirring frequently. Serve on buns.

Yield: 20 servings

Cabbage Casserole

Jill Schafer ◆ Otter Tail County

This is just like cabbage rolls, but without the work!

1 pound ground beef
1 cup onion, chopped
1 pint tomato juice
1 ¾ pounds cabbage, chopped
½ cup rice, uncooked
½ teaspoon salt
3 cloves garlic, chopped
1 pint beef broth
1 (16-ounce) jar sauerkraut, partially drained
sliced bacon

Brown ground beef and onions. Drain. Combine beef and onion with tomato juice, cabbage, uncooked rice, salt and garlic. Put in a deep casserole dish. Add beef broth, sauerkraut and place bacon strips on top.

Bake at 350° for 1 hour covered. Remove bacon and stir. Replace bacon and bake for an additional 30 minutes at 350°.

Yield: 6 to 8 servings

Kevin's Grilled Veggie Bundles

Patricia R. Swanson ◆ Pennington County

In our area, outdoor grilling is a popular "man's way" of cooking. These grilled veggies were made for family and friends by our son Kevin Alan at his home in Eagan. This recipe is submitted in loving remembrance of his hospitality.

12 small red potatoes, scrubbed and quartered with skin on
8 large carrots, cut into chunks
1 green pepper, thinly sliced (optional)
2 small onions, thinly sliced
1½ teaspoons salt
dash of pepper
3 tablespoons Parmesan cheese
⅓ cup olive oil
7 to 8 tablespoons butter or margarine

Place all vegetables, divided, onto 7 pieces of heavy-duty aluminum foil (about 12 inches square). Top with salt, pepper and cheese. Drizzle with olive oil. Top each serving with 1 tablespoon or more of butter or margarine. Fold foil up and over vegetables, sealing, leaving airspace. Do not tightly enclose vegetables. Grill over medium heat about 40 minutes (check at 30 minutes) or until vegetables are tender. Open packets carefully to allow steam to escape.

Yield: 7 bundles

Cook's Note: Kevin always served these veggies with steaks off the grill, Texas toast, pickles and various chilled beverages. Outdoor on the deck, of course!

Chicken Crescent Roll Hotdish

Peggy Metz ✦ Pope County

Chicken Filling:
½ cup onion, chopped
½ cup celery, chopped
1 tablespoon oil or butter
3 to 4 cups chicken or turkey, cooked and diced
1 can cream of mushroom or cream of chicken soup
1 (8-ounce) can of water chestnuts, sliced
⅔ cup mayonnaise
1 (4-ounce) can mushrooms, optional
½ cup sour cream
1 tube crescent roll dough

Topping:
⅔ cup Swiss cheese, shredded
3 to 4 tablespoons butter, melted
½ cup almonds, slivered

In a skillet, sauté onion and celery in 1 tablespoon oil or butter. Combine all ingredients except crescent roll dough with onions and celery. Cook over medium heat until hot and bubbly. Pour into a 9x13-inch pan; spread crescent roll dough on top.

Bake at 375° for 10 minutes. Spread with topping and bake an additional 10 to 15 minutes until golden brown.

Yield: Serves 8 to 10 people

Minnesota Dinner

Judith B. LaDuke ◆ Mahnomen County

The Ojibwe word for wild rice is *mahnomen*, sometimes spelled as *manomin*. This is where Mahnomen County and the village of Mahnomen received their names.

Natural wild rice (much better than cultivated paddy rice) is harvested by hand in mid-September. White Earth Reservation is one of the leading producers of natural wild rice in Minnesota. The rice is harvested by a two-person team in a flat-bottomed rice boat. One person stands and propels the boat through the rice plants by pushing with a long pole with a "duck bill" on the end so the pole will not sink into the bottom muck. The other person uses two sticks called "knockers," pulling the rice plant over the boat with one and pounding the plants with the other to dislodge the mature green rice kernels into the boat.

When the harvested rice is brought to shore, the green rice is parched, threshed and winnowed by traditional or mechanical means.

This recipe first appeared in the *Mahnomen Pioneer* in 1939.

1½ cups wild rice
4 slices medium thick smoked ham, finely diced
2 tablespoons lard or shortening
2 medium onions, cut fine
3 cups hot water
½ medium-sized cabbage head, cut medium-fine
2 cups tomato juice and pulp
salt, pepper and cayenne pepper to taste

Soak rice in cold water 20 minutes. Fry the diced ham in 2 tablespoons of lard or shortening until slightly browned. Add rice which has been washed and drained; stir, add onions and fry about 10 minutes, stirring until it is browned evenly.

Add the hot water and cook until water boils down, stirring constantly. In a separate kettle, cook cabbage at the same time with just enough water to cook. Mix all ingredients together including tomato juice and pulp and seasonings. Boil together until hot.

Grease a covered bean pot or earthen-ware covered dish. Place mixture in dish. Bake in a preheated oven at 350° until liquid cooks down. Serve hot.

Yield: 4 to 6 servings

Kielbasa Sausage Hotdish

Joan Serbus ◆ Clearwater County

2 pounds kielbasa sausage
1 (14- to 16-ounce) can sauerkraut
1 (10¾ ounce) can cream soup (any kind)
5 to 6 potatoes, partially cooked and cubed
1 cup sour cream
1 cup mayonnaise

Cut sausage into small pieces. Drain the sauerkraut. Place all the ingredients into a slow cooker for about 2 to 3 hours on medium.

Yield: 6 servings

Joe Lembcke's Slow Cooker Goose

Happy Hearts—Extension Home Study Group ◆ Stevens County

1 wild goose breast
1 can of beer
⅓ cup maple syrup
1 teaspoon seasoned salt
1 teaspoon garlic salt
½ teaspoon pepper

Put all ingredients in a slow cooker. Cook for 6 hours on low. Check for tenderness and enjoy; or, if needed, cook a couple hours longer.

Yield: 4 to 6 servings

Jankee Chili

Joanna Alcott ◆ Becker County

This chili makes a great "help-yourself" meal. It's quick and easy, and you can make it the day before. For a hot, healthy meal, just add a salad. When there's sickness, a funeral, new baby – whatever the occasion – I like to take this to the family because everyone seems to like it, and it keeps well.

1 pound ground beef
1 medium onion, chopped
½ teaspoon garlic salt
salt and pepper to taste
1 (10¾-ounce) can vegetable beef soup
1 (10¾-ounce) can condensed tomato soup
1 soup can water
1 can kidney beans, undrained
1½ cup macaroni, cooked (about ⅔ cup dry)
1½ tablespoons chili powder
1 tablespoon vinegar
1 tablespoon brown sugar

In large saucepan or very large fry pan, brown ground beef, onion and garlic salt. Add a little salt and pepper. Stir to separate hamburger and then add the rest of the ingredients. Simmer 30 minutes; stir occasionally.

Yield: 6 to 8 servings

Cook's Note: If chili gets too thick, just add a little water.

Traverse County 4-H Chili

Anne Hanson ◆ Traverse County

E very family in Traverse County has a favorite recipe but each one has a special touch that produces the taste we assume everybody wants. If you doubt that truth, ask any family what goes into meatballs or tater tot hotdish. The Traverse County fair has been a major tradition with the unique distinction of being held the weekend after Labor Day. I suspect that timeframe fit with small-grain harvest that began after the fair. Harvest season and the Traverse County Fair time have changed, but the county 4-Hers still serve chili that tastes the same as everybody remembers from their first visit to the fair. Nobody remembers who developed the recipe. We just call it the 4-H recipe.

2½ pounds ground beef
1½ cups celery, diced
2 cups onion, diced
3 teaspoons salt
½ teaspoon pepper
1 (46-ounce) can tomato juice
½ cup water
1 tablespoon chili powder
1½ cups ketchup
1 teaspoon dry mustard
1 gallon kidney beans, undrained

Brown ground beef, stirring until crumbly; drain. Add celery and onions to ground beef mixture and cook until tender. Add remaining ingredients and simmer until desired consistency.

Yield: 1½ gallons

Wild Rice Pheasant Casserole

Janine Lovold ◆ Roseau County

Our area has pheasant shooting preserves that draw hunters; the wild rice is grown within 100 miles of our county.

2 cups wild rice, cooked (⅔ cup dry)
1 cup carrot strips, cooked, cooled and cut into 1-inch strips
5 slices bacon
1 to 2 tablespoons oil
2 skinless, boneless pheasant breast halves,
   cut into 2x2-inch pieces
salt and pepper to taste
5 medium mushrooms, sliced
5 green onions, sliced
1 (10¾-ounce) can cream of chicken soup
¼ cup cream or milk
¼ cup sherry or dry white wine
1 cup mozzarella cheese, shredded
1 (14-ounce) can artichoke hearts, drained and quartered
¼ cup Parmesan cheese, grated

Put the cooked and cooled wild rice into a 9-inch square baking dish that has been sprayed with nonstick vegetable spray. Layer the cooled carrots over the wild rice.

In a large skillet, cook bacon until crisp; drain and crumble over the carrots. Pour off grease from skillet and add 1 to 2 tablespoons oil. Sauté the pheasant until well browned on both sides (about 10 minutes.) Season with salt and pepper. Transfer pheasant to baking dish.

In the same skillet, sauté the mushrooms and green onions until tender; adding more oil if needed. Add soup, cream and sherry; mix well. Add mozzarella and gently stir in the artichokes. Spread over pheasant layer. Sprinkle with Parmesan cheese. Cover dish with foil sprayed with nonstick vegetable spray. Bake in a preheated oven at 350° for 30 minutes; remove foil and bake 15 more minutes until bubbly.

Yield: 4 to 5 servings

Boiled Raisin Cupcakes

Janice Ellingson ◆ Grant County

This recipe is from my Aunt Helen, who was married to long-time state Rep. Carl M. Iverson. The recipe originated from her mother, Hannah Melby Ellingson, who was the daughter of a Civil War veteran. He homesteaded in the northeast corner of Grant County soon after that war.

Cupcakes:
  2 cups hot water
  2 cups sugar
  2 cups raisins
  1 cup lard or shortening
  1 teaspoon cloves
  1 teaspoon salt
  2 teaspoons cinnamon
  3 eggs, beaten lightly
  1 teaspoon vanilla
  3 cups flour (can use 2 cups cake flour
     and 1 cup all-purpose)
  1 teaspoon soda
  1 teaspoon baking powder

Frosting:
  1 cup sugar
  ¾ cup brown sugar, packed
  ¾ cup half-and-half
  1 teaspoon vanilla

Cupcakes: In 2 cups hot water, boil sugar, raisins, lard, cloves, salt and cinnamon for about 15 minutes. Cool. Add eggs and vanilla to the cooled mixture; blend in the dry ingredients which have been sifted together. Fill muffin cups ⅔ full. Bake in a preheated oven at 350° for 12 to 15 minutes or until toothpick inserted in center comes out clean.

Frosting: Boil sugars and half-and-half until soft ball stage when tested in cold water. Add vanilla and beat until ready to spread.

Scandinavian Almond Cake

Rachel Barduson ◆ Douglas County

What makes this particular recipe so special is the shape of the cake pan. It measures about 12 inches long and has a rounded, fluted bottom – found in Scandinavian shops. In Scandinavian cooking, the shape was and still is important. Although this cake is a very old, basic dessert, it's one of the most popular items served at the Douglas County Historical Society and sold at our Ethnic Bake Sale. People love the almond flavor. It's especially festive at Christmas.

> sliced almonds, optional
> 1 ¼ cups sugar
> 1 egg
> 1 ½ teaspoons pure almond extract
> ⅔ cup milk
> 1 ¼ cups flour
> ½ teaspoon baking powder
> 1 stick butter or margarine, melted
> powdered sugar

Preheat oven to 350°. Spray special loaf pan with cooking spray. Before pouring batter into the pan, you may sprinkle sliced almonds on the bottom. Beat the sugar, egg, almond extract and milk. Add flour and baking powder and mix with mixer. Add melted butter. Mix well. Bake for 40 to 50 minutes. Edges must be golden brown. Cool in pan before removing. Cake will break if removed too soon. Sprinkle with powdered sugar.

Yield: Makes 1 loaf pan

Cook's Note: It's very important to "know your oven" when baking this cake because it can be touchy. Edges must be golden brown, but be sure the center is completely baked. Let cool before inverting the pan and placing on a beautiful cake platter.

Butterscotch Nut Torte

Kally Glander ◆ Wilkin County

I made this recipe with my grandma, MaryAnn Melcher, when I was young. It's become a family favorite that we usually serve at the holidays.

Cake:
 6 eggs, separated
 1½ cups sugar
 1 teaspoon baking powder
 1 teaspoon almond extract
 2 teaspoons vanilla extract
 1 cup walnuts, broken
 2 cups graham cracker crumbs

Topping:
 1 pint whipping cream
 3 tablespoons powdered sugar

Sauce:
 1 cup brown sugar, packed
 ¼ cup orange juice
 ¼ cup butter
 1 egg, well beaten
 ½ cup water
 ½ teaspoon vanilla extract
 1 tablespoon flour

Cake: Beat egg yolks well; add sugar, baking powder and extracts. Beat egg whites until they form peaks. Fold egg whites into yolk mixture. Add cracker crumbs and then add nuts. Pour into a greased 9x13x2-inch baking pan. Bake in a preheated oven at 325° for 30 minutes. Cool completely.

Topping: Whip cream along with powdered sugar until stiff peaks form; spread on top of cake.

Sauce: To make sauce, combine ingredients in a saucepan and mix well. Bring to a boil until thick; let cool. Place cake on serving plate and top with sauce.

Yield: 15 servings

Dark Icebox Cookies

Linda Houglum ◆ Norman County

These spicy cookies originally were made with bacon drippings, but I've substituted trans fat-free shortening or butter. They're nice with afternoon coffee or on a cookie tray.

⅔ cup shortening	½ teaspoon cloves
2 cups brown sugar, packed	1 teaspoon ginger
2 eggs	1 teaspoon nutmeg
½ cup molasses	1 ½ teaspoons baking soda
2 tablespoons cream	1 teaspoon salt
2 teaspoons cinnamon	4 cups flour

Mix shortening, brown sugar, eggs, molasses and cream. Add dry ingredients; mix well. Form into 3 12-inch rolls. Wrap rolls with wax paper and chill.

Cut into ¼-inch to ⅛-inch slices and place on cookie sheet. Bake in a preheated oven at 350° for approximately 10 minutes.

Yield: About 9 dozen cookies

Chocolate Cherry Bars

Patty Benson ◆ Grant County

Bars are a popular dessert to bring to potlucks and other gatherings. This recipe is quick and easy and fits into our busy schedules.

Bars:	**Frosting:**
1 box chocolate cake mix	1 cup sugar
1 (21-ounce) can cherry pie filling	5 tablespoon butter or margarine
1 teaspoon almond extract	⅓ cup milk
2 eggs, beaten	1 cup chocolate chips

Bars: Mix cake mix, pie filling, almond extract and eggs by hand in a large bowl. Pour into a greased jelly roll pan. Bake in a preheated oven at 350° degrees for 30 minutes. Let cool.

Frosting: In a saucepan, mix sugar, butter and milk. Bring to a boil. Boil 1 minute. Remove from heat. Add chocolate chips. Stir until chips are melted and frosting is smooth. Frost cooled bars.

Yield: About 20 servings

Ginger Creams

Carol Hugill Taggart—in memory of Amelia Diamond Hugill
◆ Kittson County

This is a soft cookie and very different from gingersnaps.

½ cup butter	2¾ cups flour
1 cup sugar	½ teaspoon cinnamon
½ cup dark molasses	½ teaspoon ginger
2 eggs beaten	½ teaspoon ground cloves
½ cup very hot coffee	½ teaspoon salt
1 teaspoon baking soda	

Cream the butter, sugar and molasses. Beat in eggs, coffee and soda. Sift flour, cinnamon, ginger, cloves and salt together. Mix into the butter mixture. Chill dough for one hour. Then, using a tablespoon, drop cookies onto greased cookie sheet. Bake in a preheated oven at 350º for 12 to 13 minutes.

Yield: 4 to 5 dozen cookies

Cook's Note: Can be frosted with your favorite vanilla frosting.

My Most-Requested Sugar Cookies

Renee Schwebach ◆ Traverse County

I bake these for all the holidays and either frost them and put sprinkles on top or decorate them with egg yolk "paint" before they are baked. They are very rich because they're made with butter. When I was young, my dad milked cows, and my husband and his family were in dairy, too. So the rich goodness of dairy products will forever be a part of my baking.

One Halloween, I baked 83 dozen! They were sold to co-workers, sold at the bake sale at our church bazaar, given as treats and eaten by my family.

Many batches of these sugar cookies found their way to our daughter, Jamie, this past year when she served with the Army Reserves in Kuwait and Iraq. She shared them with fellow soldiers, and they were enjoyed by everyone.

Cookies:
1 cup butter, softened
1 ½ cups powdered sugar
1 egg
1 teaspoon vanilla
1 teaspoon almond flavoring
2 ½ cups flour

Egg Yolk Paint:
1 egg yolk
2 teaspoons water
2 teaspoons corn syrup
paste coloring

Cookies: Mix butter, sugar, egg, vanilla and almond flavoring together well. Blend in flour. Cover; chill for 3 hours.

Divide dough in half. Roll about ¼-inch thick on a floured surface. Cut with cookie cutters. Paint with Egg Yolk Paint, if desired, and bake in a preheated oven at 350° for about 10 minutes or until edges begin to turn brown. Cool. Frost or leave plain.

Egg Yolk Paint: Take 1 egg yolk; use half of it. Add water and corn syrup. Mix well. Stir in paste coloring until you get the color you want. Using a paint brush, paint designs on the cookies before you bake them.

Yield: 3 dozen

Krumb Kaka

Caryl J. Bugge ◆ Pennington County

This recipe, a traditional Norwegian cookie, was given to me by one of my mother's friends, Linda Merritt.

½ cup butter, melted
1 ½ cups sugar
3 eggs
½ teaspoon vanilla
1 cup sour cream
2 cups flour

Cream melted butter with sugar. Add remaining ingredients. Beat until smooth. Let rest for 30 minutes or more. (If more than 30 minutes, let chill in the refrigerator.)

Heat Krumb Kaka iron on medium heat (or on a one-burner hot-plate). Drop a small teaspoon of the batter on the iron, press down for 30 seconds, turn and heat for 30 seconds, remove with a metal spatula, and roll immediately.

Yield: Approximately 5 dozen

Cook's Note: This recipe takes approximately 2 hours and requires your undivided attention.

Rosettes

Don Nasstrom ◆ Clay County

This is a very pretty, delicate Norwegian cookie that's great with coffee and as a gift for friends.

> 3 eggs, beaten
> 3 teaspoons sugar
> 2 cups whole milk
> 2 cups flour
> 1 pound shortening
> sugar

Mix together thoroughly eggs, sugar, milk and flour. Melt shortening in deep fat fryer and heat to 350°. Dip the rosette iron in fat and then into batter. Fry until golden – tap iron to release cookie, dip in sugar. Store in cool dry place.

Yield: 4 to 5 dozen

Pear Pie

Neva Foster ◆ Big Stone County

> 1 pastry for double crust pie
> 6 pears, peeled and sliced
> 1 cup sugar
> 1 tablespoon lemon juice
> 2 tablespoons flour
> ¼ to ½ teaspoon nutmeg

Mix pears, sugar, lemon juice and flour and place in crust, then sprinkle nutmeg over the pears. Cover with top crust and bake in a preheated oven at 350° for 1 to 1¼ hours.

Yield: 1 pie

Rommegrot Bars

Phyllis Erickson ◆ Pope County

Rommegrot is a popular Norwegian dish, and these bars are another way to enjoy it.

Filling:
12 ounces cream cheese, softened
(add up to 6 ounces more if you like)
1 cup sugar
1 egg yolk

Crust:
2 packages crescent rolls

Topping:
1 egg white
¾ cup fresh walnuts, finely chopped
⅓ cup sugar
½ teaspoon cinnamon

Filling: Mix cream cheese, sugar and egg yolk; beat well.

Crust: Spread 1 package of crescent rolls in a 9x13-inch pan to the edges. Spread filling over rolls. Layer second package of rolls over filling, edge to edge.

Topping: Beat egg white slightly, spread over crust. Sprinkle walnuts. Combine sugar and cinnamon. Sprinkle over nuts. Bake in a preheated oven at 350° for 30 minutes.

Yield: 15 to 20 bars

Sandbakkelse

Diane Rapacz ✦ Polk County

The community where I grew up and live in now is widely Scandinavian. I am very proud of my heritage, and try to preserve it with recipes my grandmother gave me. I have so many wonderful memories making these special treats with her! To recreate those memories, my husband and I invite our nieces, nephews and our friends' children to our home to bake these Scandinavian cookies. We serve pizza, play a game, and then they wrap the cookies and take them home to their parents for Christmas.

Although we usually serve these cookies during the holidays, they're delicious all year 'round!

> 1 pound butter, softened
> 1 cup sugar
> 1 egg
> ½ teaspoon almond extract
> 2¾ to 3 cups flour

Cream butter and sugar together. Add the egg and almond extract; mix well. Mix in flour to make a very stiff dough.

Press dough into sandbakkel tins, trim edges, and bake at 375° degrees for 15 minutes. Allow to cool for a short time before removing from tins.

Cook's Note: I start with a good amount of dough in the bottom of the tin and then work it up around the sides with my thumbs while turning the tin at the same time. Kids catch on quick – it's so much fun to see their excitement when they do their first one!

Glorified Rhubarb Rice

Anne Hanson ◆ Traverse County

Rhubarb, pie plant, weed – call it what you like, but Minnesota is rhubarb country. The tart stalks are old-fashioned summer treats when pulled right from the plant and sprinkled with salt.

> 5 cups rhubarb, cut in 1-inch pieces
> 1 cup sugar
> 1 (6-ounce) package strawberry gelatin
> 1 package frozen strawberries
> 1 cup long grain rice
> salt, to taste
> 1 tablespoon sugar
> 1 cup whipping cream
> marshmallows, optional
> fresh strawberries, optional

Cook rhubarb and 1 cup sugar in microwave until rhubarb is soft. Stir in strawberry gelatin. Add frozen strawberries. Cool in refrigerator.

Cook long grain rice, then stir in salt and tablespoon of sugar. Cool thoroughly. Whip cream and stir into rice. Add rhubarb sauce. Add marshmallows and fresh cut strawberries, if desired. Adjust amount of cream and sugar to taste.

Yield: 8 to 12 servings

Rhubarb Crunch

Shirley Gunderson ◆ Clearwater County

I n early spring, we can't wait for the rhubarb to get big enough for this dessert!

Crust:
    1 ½ cups flour
    1 ½ cups brown sugar, packed
    1 ¼ cups oatmeal
    ¾ cup butter, softened
    1 teaspoon cinnamon

Filling:
    1 ½ cups sugar
    3 tablespoons cornstarch
    1 ½ cups water
    1 ½ teaspoons vanilla
    6 cups rhubarb, diced
    1 (21-ounce) can cherry pie filling

Crust: Preheat oven to 350°. Mix the crust ingredients. Put ½ in a 9x13-inch glass cake pan. Top with filling and then top with remaining crust mixture. Bake for 1 hour.

Filling: Combine sugar and cornstarch, add water and cook until mixture comes to a boil. Add vanilla, rhubarb and cherry pie filling.

Yield: 10 to 12 servings

Tin Can Ice Cream

Lynnette Price ◆ Becker County

This recipe is fun for the kids — and the kid in us!

> 1 cup whole milk
> ½ cup sugar
> 1 cup whipping cream
> ½ teaspoon real vanilla extract

Place all ingredients in a 1-pound coffee can with a tight-fitting plastic lid. Put the 1-pound can filled with its ingredients inside a 3-pound can. Pack large can with crushed ice (or we use snow here in the Minnesota winter months) and pour at least ¾ cup rock salt over the ice. Place lid on large can.

Roll can back and forth on floor for 10 minutes. Open large can and drain off water and add additional ice (or snow) and salt. Roll an additional 5 minutes. It's ready!

Yield: 5 servings

Cook's Note: Instead of using the 1- and 3-pound coffee cans, you can use 1-quart and 1-gallon heavy-duty zippered plastic bags, and shake.

Muskadee Special Pie

Lilly Saker & Jan Nelson ✦ Clay County

Richard Saker was section foreman at the Northern Pacific railway station at Muskoda (pronounced Mus-ka-dee) in Clay County from 1946 to 1954. His wife, Lilly, made and served this pie at the station and continued to make it when they were transferred to Duluth. Lilly's nephew, Alden Anderson, donated this recipe to the Clay County Museum in 2006. Jan Nelson, a volunteer and co-worker, updated the ingredients and instructions.

Crust:
15 graham crackers, crushed
¼ cup butter, melted, optional

Filling:
22 marshmallows
½ cup milk
½ ounce baking chocolate, cut in small pieces
¼ cup maraschino cherries, cut up
¼ cup walnuts, chopped
1 cup whipping cream, whipped

Crust: Mix graham crackers and butter, press into 8- or 9-inch pie tin.

Filling: Melt marshmallows and milk in double boiler; let cool. Add chocolate, cherries, nuts and cream. Mix well and pour into pie crust. Refrigerate until ready to serve.

Yield: 6 to 8 servings

NORTHEAST REGION

Blueberries and wild rice, venison and rabbit, wild mushrooms and walleye. Nature's pantry has inspired Northwoods cooks from the earliest Native Americans to today's five-star chefs. Immigrants from Eastern Europe, Germany, Scandinavia and France brought their hearty pasties, soups, chowders and stroganoffs with them to their new communities nestled among the region's forests, meadows, lakes and the ore-rich mountains of the Iron Range.

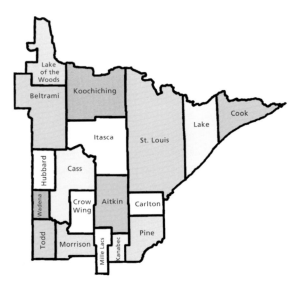

Wassail

Brenda Yancey ♦ Lake of the Woods County

This is the perfect drink to have at all of your Minnesota winter activities: skating rink, sledding hill, snowmobiling trail, ice fishing house, hockey game and hunting shack. And it makes your house smell like the holidays!

    3 quarts water
    3 cups sugar
    8 whole cinnamon sticks
    8 whole allspice berries
    24 whole cloves
    ¾ teaspoon ginger
    1 gallon apple cider
    6 cups orange juice
    ½ cup lemon juice
    3 cups water

Combine 3 quarts water, sugar, cinnamon, allspice, cloves and ginger in a large pot. Bring to a boil and simmer for 2 hours. Add remaining ingredients and return to a boil.

Yield: About 2 gallons

Omelet in a Baggie

Jean Badovinac ♦ Itasca County

This recipe is fun for kids and company.

    2 large eggs
    1 tablespoon of your favorite cheese, shredded
    1 tablespoon chopped ham, cooked bacon, mushrooms
     or other filling ingredients (optional)
    1 freezer zippered plastic bag (1 quart)
    boiling water

Break eggs into a small mixing bowl. Using a wire whisk or a fork, lightly beat eggs. Add cheese and filling ingredient(s) and stir to combine. Carefully pour egg mixture into zippered bag. Seal bag then open seal about 1-inch and press to remove air from bag. Reseal firmly.

Fill a 2-quart saucepan about ⅔ full with water. Cover and place on heat; bring to a full boil. Place the filled zippered bag into boiling water. Boil egg mixture for 5 minutes. Using tongs, carefully remove the zippered bag from the water. Open the bag and roll the omelet onto a plate. When the omelet is done it slides easily out of the bag.

Yield: 1 serving

Cook's Note: Make sure the plastic bag is a heavy-duty freezer bag.

Soft Herbed Cheese Spread

Brook Berg ◆ Hubbard County

This is a favorite at our house and with our guests.

2 cloves garlic, minced
2 sticks butter, softened
12 ounces cream cheese
¼ teaspoon basil
¼ teaspoon marjoram
¼ teaspoon dill
¼ teaspoon thyme
crackers or fresh veggies

With the blade running in the food processor, drop in the garlic cloves. Then combine butter and cream cheese. Add seasonings and mix in processor until smooth. Refrigerate.

Yield: 16 servings

Cook's Note: We serve this spread with chicken, as well as crackers, bread and fruit. Keeps 1 month or can be frozen.

Breakfast Burritos

Barb Cowan—Innkeeper at LoonSong B & B ◆ Hubbard County

Wˢe make this homestyle breakfast at LoonSong B & B. It has a zesty, snappy taste that will start your day with a smile!

Burritos:
- 1 pound ground pork sausage
- ¼ cup onion, diced
- ¼ cup green pepper, diced
- 1½ cups frozen southern style hash brown potatoes
- 4 eggs, beaten
- 12 (8-inch) flour tortillas
- ½ cup Cheddar cheese, shredded
- picante sauce, spicy bean salsa and sour cream, optional

Spicy Bean Salsa:
- 1 (15-ounce) can black-eyed peas
- 1 (15-ounce) can of black peas, drained and rinsed
- 1 (15-ounce) can whole kernel corn, drained
- ½ cup onion, chopped
- ½ cup green bell pepper, diced
- 1 (4-ounce) can diced jalapeno peppers
- 1 (14½-ounce) can of diced tomatoes, drained
- 1 cup Italian dressing
- ½ teaspoon garlic salt
- ⅓ cup fresh cilantro, chopped

Burritos: Brown sausage in large skillet. Add the onion and pepper, cook until tender. Add potatoes and cook until tender, about 8 minutes. Add beaten eggs; stir. Cook until eggs are completely set. Warm tortillas and spoon mixture down the center of tortillas; sprinkle with cheese. Fold sides in and roll to enclose filling. Serve with picante sauce, spicy bean salsa and sour cream.

Spicy Bean Salsa: Combine black-eyed peas, black peas, whole kernel corn, onion, green bell pepper, jalapeno peppers and diced tomatoes. Add Italian dressing, garlic salt and cilantro, mix well. Cover and refrigerate overnight. Makes 4 cups. Refrigerate after serving, will keep for several weeks.

Yield: 12 servings

Cook's Note: I always make a double batch of these burritos – one for eating now and one for freezing. Wrap each burrito separately and freeze; just pop them into microwave for a fast breakfast anytime. Serve the salsa over the burritos or with tortilla chips.

Caramelized French Toast

Lake County Historical Society and Light House B & B ◆ Lake County

Our guests rave about this breakfast dish.

> ½ cup butter
> 1 cup brown sugar, packed
> 2 tablespoons light corn syrup
> 12 slices English muffin bread
> apple butter, optional
> 6 eggs, beaten
> 1¼ cups milk
> 1 teaspoon vanilla
> ¼ teaspoon salt

Lightly spray/grease a 9x13-inch baking pan. In medium saucepan, mix butter, brown sugar and corn syrup. Heat until melted and smooth. Pour into baking pan. Layer bread slices over top. (Can also spread a layer of apple butter between bread slices.) Beat remaining ingredients just until blended. Pour over bread. Seal pan tightly and refrigerate overnight. Uncover, place in cold oven. Bake at 350° for 40 to 60 minutes.

Yield: Approximately 6 servings

Cook's Note: We serve the French toast with seasonal fruit and bacon, ham or breakfast sausage.

Apple Streusel Muffins

Mary and Marty Raddatz ◆ Todd County

Muffins:
 1½ cups flour
 ¼ cup sugar
 2 teaspoons baking powder
 ½ teaspoon cinnamon
 ¼ teaspoon salt
 ⅛ teaspoon nutmeg
 1 egg
 ½ cup milk
 ¼ cup vegetable oil
 1 cup tart apples (Haralson), finely chopped and peeled

Streusel Topping:
 ⅓ cup brown sugar, packed
 2 tablespoons flour
 ½ teaspoon cinnamon
 2 tablespoons butter, softened
 ⅓ cup pecans, chopped

Muffins: In large bowl, combine flour, sugar, baking powder, cinnamon, salt and nutmeg. In a small bowl, beat the egg, milk and oil. Stir mixture into dry ingredients until moistened. Fold in apples.

Streusel Topping: In another small bowl, combine topping ingredients. Set aside 3 tablespoons topping.

Spoon half of the batter into 12 greased muffin cups. Sprinkle with topping. Cover with additional batter to fill muffin cups ⅔ full. Sprinkle with reserved topping. Bake in a preheated oven at 400° for 20 to 25 minutes or until a wooden pick inserted at the center comes out clean. Cool for 5 minutes before removing from pan to a wire rack.

Yield: 12 muffins

Blueberry Muffins

John Wallin ◆ Crow Wing County

Blueberries are nature's champs when it comes to antioxidant and anti-inflammatory properties. With our society growing older, we're looking for foods that will help keep us healthier and more alert. Many sources report blueberry benefits including improved vision, stronger blood vessels and clearer arteries, disease protection, enhanced memory, reduced urinary tract infections and better weight control.

½ cup butter or margarine
1 ¼ cups sugar
2 eggs
1 cup sour cream or plain yogurt
1 teaspoon vanilla
1 teaspoon baking powder
½ teaspoon baking soda
¼ teaspoon salt
2 cups flour
2 cups blueberries

Preheat oven to 375°. Cream butter and sugar, add eggs and beat until smooth. Mix in sour cream and vanilla. Combine dry ingredients and stir into creamed mixture. Fold in blueberries. Spoon into muffin tins that are either lined with paper liners or sprayed with oil. Bake until golden brown, about 25 to 35 minutes.

Yield: 16 large or 18 medium muffins

Cook's Note: Blueberry muffins are the official Minnesota state muffin!

Grandma's Cinnamon Rolls

Faythe Kinnunen ◆ Wadena County

This recipe offers a taste of Americana from rural Minnesota. Our family has enjoyed them over and over. I freeze most of the cinnamon rolls and take out a bag when needed. I always have extra for when people come visit. They make great gifts for birthdays and other holidays, especially since not many people bake anymore.

Part of our house is more than 100 years old. The kitchen has seen quite a few changes. The wood-burning kitchen range gave way to a gas stove, and now we have an electric range. It's much easier cooking and baking now! At one time there was a "summer kitchen" where all the cooking and eating was done during the warm weather.

2 cups water, hot
½ cup powdered milk
½ cup sugar
2 teaspoons salt
2 packages yeast, approximately 2 tablespoons
   if using bulk yeast
2 eggs
½ cup shortening
7 to 8 cups flour
butter or margarine, melted
3 tablespoons sugar
1 tablespoon cinnamon

Put hot water, powdered milk, sugar, salt and shortening into a bowl. Mix; then add 2 cups flour and yeast. Mix well. Add 1 more cup flour and eggs; mix well. Work in rest of flour and knead until smooth. I put the dough in a large plastic bowl and place it into the sink with a couple inches of hot water in the sink. Cover the dough with a towel–this helps it raise regardless of the temperature of the kitchen.

After the dough has risen (doubled in size) punch it down and let it rise again. After it has risen the second time roll out ½ the dough on a flat surface (with a little flour on it to keep the dough from sticking to it) about 9 inches wide and 18 inches long. Spread with melted butter or margarine. Combine sugar and cinnamon and sprinkle on the rolled out dough. Roll the dough into one long roll; cut each roll with string or dental floss instead of a knife and place onto a greased pan. Repeat with the other half of the dough.

Bake in a preheated oven at 425° for 15 to 20 minutes.

Yield: 3 to 4 dozen rolls

Cook's Note: When I take the rolls from the oven, I brush them with water because this keeps the crust softer.

Yogurt Muffins
Lake County Historical Society and
Lighthouse B & B ◆ Lake County

2 cups flour
⅔ cup sugar
1 teaspoon baking powder
1 teaspoon baking soda
¼ cup oil
1 egg
1 (8-ounce) container yogurt — your choice
2 cups fruit, chopped — your choice
12 teaspoons wheat germ, one teaspoon for each muffin top

Preheat oven to 350°. Sift together flour, sugar, baking powder and baking soda. Add oil, egg and yogurt. Mix just until blended. Fold in fruit. Grease or spray muffin pan. Spoon batter ⅔ full into muffin pans. Top each with a teaspoon of wheat germ. Bake for 20 minutes.

Yield: 12 muffins

Cook's Note: Popular fruit and yogurt combinations for these muffins are lemon yogurt and blueberries, peach yogurt and diced peaches and vanilla yogurt and sliced strawberries.

Pork and Bean Bread

Norma Weinzierl ◆ Crow Wing County

I entered this recipe some years ago at the Bean Hole Days festival in Pequot Lakes and won first place. This celebration is a big activity in Crow Wing County and draws many people to the area in the summer. This recipe is a great conversation piece.

1 cup raisins	1 teaspoon vanilla
1 cup water, boiling	3 eggs
2 cups sugar	1 cup oil
3 cups flour	1 teaspoon cinnamon
1 cup nuts	½ teaspoon soda
1 (16-ounce) can of pork and beans	½ teaspoon salt

Soak the raisins in boiling water, set aside. Mix all other ingredients. Drain raisins and add to mixture. Put in 3 greased loaf pans. Bake in a preheated oven at 350° for 1 hour.

Yield: 3 loaves

Milch Bróte (Milk Bread)

Brenda Meyer ◆ Morrison County

My mother, Leona Welle, grew up on a dairy farm in eastern Morrison County. My father also grew up on a dairy farm 2½ miles away. They fell in love and got married during the Armistice Day Blizzard of 1940. While the wedding party was getting their pictures taken in another town, my parents became stranded on the road. Their borrowed car caught fire and had to be put out with snow! After they went to a farmhouse for food and shelter, one of the local farmers came with his horse and wagon to bring them back to town. My parents never made it to their own wedding reception and spent the next three days at my aunt and uncle's house.

My mother and father built their own farm between their parents' places and spent the rest of their lives there. Saturday was always baking day. The family looked forward to this special treat, and I make it to this day because it brings back such special memories.

> ⅓ cup milk
> ⅓ cup cream
> ¼ cup sugar
> 1 to 2 tablespoons cinnamon
> 1 pound bread dough or 1 loaf frozen bread dough, thawed

Pour milk and cream in the bottom of an 8-inch square baking pan so it is about ½ inch deep. Add sugar and lots of cinnamon (1 or 2 table-spoons, to your taste). Mix well in pan. Cut small chunks of bread dough and put in pan on top of mixture. Press down lightly.

Let rise for ½ hour. Bake at 350° degrees until golden brown. Serve warm.

Yield: 1 (8-inch) pan

Hungarian Pottage Soup

Mustang Steak House ♦ Kanabec County

This soup has been prepared by Sandy in Mora for 20 years.

1 pound ground beef, browned	½ cup mushrooms, sliced
1 cup potatoes, diced	¼ cup ketchup
1 cup carrots, chopped	2 tablespoons beef base
1 cup celery, chopped	1 teaspoon garlic salt
1 cup onion, chopped	1 gallon water
½ cup green peppers, chopped	½ cup vegetable oil
	1 cup flour

Mix all ingredients except oil and flour. Simmer for 1 hour. Mix oil and flour together with a wire whisk. Add to soup, stirring continuously until creamy.

Yield: 1 gallon

This Stuff Should Win A Prize!

Betty Birnstihl ✦ **St. Louis County**

I have never shared this recipe because I always thought I should enter it in a contest, thus the name. It's an easy, delicious, yeasty coffee cake that is best when still warm.

Base:
¼ cup warm water
1 package yeast
1 cup milk
⅓ cup sugar
⅓ cup butter
1 teaspoon salt
1 egg
3½ to 4 cups flour

Filling:
3 cups blueberries (Minnesota wild berries are best)
2 tablespoons water
2 tablespoons lemon juice
3 tablespoons flour
6 tablespoons sugar

Frosting:
3 ounces cream cheese, softened
¼ cup butter, softened
1 tablespoon milk
1 teaspoon vanilla
1½ cups powdered sugar

Base: Dissolve yeast in water. Heat together milk, sugar, butter and salt until warm. Stir in 1 cup flour. Add yeast and egg. Add enough remaining flour to make a soft dough. Knead well. Place in oiled bowl, cover and let rise until doubled. Punch down, divide dough in half and let rest 10 minutes to regain elasticity. With a rolling pin roll first portion to 9x13-inch rectangle, place in greased 9x13-inch pan. Spread with filling. Roll remaining dough and place on top. Make large slits in top dough. Let rise. Bake in a preheated oven at 375° for 35 minutes (may have to cover with foil last 10 minutes.) Frost while slightly warm.

Filling: Combine blueberries, water and lemon juice in a saucepan and simmer for 2 minutes. Add flour and sugar, simmer, stirring until thickened. Cool to room temperature.

Frosting: Mix everything together and spread on bread while slightly warm.

Yield: 9x13-inch pan

Debby's Shredded Wheat Buns

Deb Schey ◆ Crow Wing County

I grew up on a farm in central Minnesota with a mother who balanced a full-time teaching career with caring for her family and making delicious home-cooked meals. She made wonderful bread, and I wanted to be like her. So years ago I began experimenting with bread. Even though I've tried many kinds, this recipe has become a tradition and a family favorite. My great-niece Hannah affectionately named these "Debby's Buns." I finally entered them at our county fair and to my delight – and my family's – I won a blue ribbon.

2 shredded wheat biscuits	¼ cup sugar
2 cups boiling water	¼ cup light molasses
2 tablespoons butter	1½ teaspoons kosher salt
1 package yeast	5 to 6 cups bread flour
(2¼ teaspoons)	butter
½ cup warm water	

Crumble shredded wheat biscuits into bowl. Add boiling water and butter. Dissolve yeast in warm water and add to wheat mixture. Add sugar, molasses, salt and flour. Mix well. Knead on a floured board until smooth (10 minutes.) Place in a greased bowl. Cover with plastic wrap and let double in size (60 to 90 minutes.) If time permits, punch dough to deflate and let rise a second time (approximately 30 minutes.) You can make 2 loaves or 2 9x13-inch pans of rolls. Let rise for 30 minutes. Bake in a preheated oven at 375° until browned, approximately 30 to 45 minutes. Remove from oven and brush with butter.

Yield: 2 loaves or 24 rolls

Wild Rice Three Grain Bread

Carol Jensen ◆ Aitkin County

Wild rice grows in lots of the lakes in our area. This is a great bread to serve with meals, to make sandwiches or to give as a gift.

1 package active dry yeast
⅓ cup warm water, 105° to 115°
2 cups milk, scalded, cooled to 105° to 115°
2 tablespoons canola or vegetable oil
1½ teaspoons salt
½ cup honey*
½ cup uncooked rolled oats
½ cup rye flour
2 cups whole wheat flour
4 to 4½ cups bread flour
1 cup cooked wild rice
1 egg, beaten with 1 tablespoon water
½ cup hulled sunflower seeds

*may use molasses instead of honey

In a large bowl, dissolve yeast in water. Add milk, oil, salt and honey. Stir in oats, rye flour, whole wheat flour and 2 cups of the bread flour to make a soft dough. Add wild rice. Cover and let rest 15 minutes. Stir in enough additional bread flour to make a stiff dough.

Turn out onto bread board and knead 10 minutes. Add more flour to keep dough from sticking. Turn dough into lightly greased bowl, turn over, cover and let rise until doubled, about 1 hour. Punch down.

Divide dough into 3 equal parts and shape into strands, then braid and place onto greased baking sheet to make a wreath. Or, divide dough into 2 equal parts and place into 9½x5½-inch greased bread pans.

Let rise until doubled, about 45 minutes. Brush tops of loaves with egg mixed with water. Slash loaves if desired. Sprinkle with sunflower seeds. Bake in a pre-heated over at 375º for 30 to 45 minutes or until loaves sound hollow when tapped.

Yield: One braided wreath or 2 pan loaves

Cheddar Chowder

Brenda Dorow ◆ Lake of the Woods County

This is a classic for hunting season. Everyone comes in for lunch when it's Cheddar Chowder!

Vegetable Broth:
2 cups water
2 cups potatoes, diced
½ cup carrots, diced
½ cup celery, diced
¼ cup onion, chopped
1 teaspoon salt
¼ teaspoon pepper

Cheese Sauce:
¼ cup butter
¼ cup flour
2 cups milk
2 cups Cheddar cheese, grated

1 cup cooked ham, diced

Vegetable Broth: Combine in large saucepan water, potatoes, carrots, celery, onion, salt and pepper. Boil for 10 to 12 minutes.

Cheese Sauce: In a medium sauce pan, make cheese sauce by melting butter, add flour and stir until smooth (about 1 minute). Slowly add milk; stir constantly. Cook until thickened. Add grated cheese and stir until cheese melts.
    Add cheese sauce and ham to the vegetable broth and heat through.

Yield: 6 servings

Cook's Note: Serve Cheddar Chowder with fresh buns and fruit.

Cheesy Wild Rice Soup

Leanna Hasbargen ◆ Koochiching County

This delicious soup will warm even the coldest night in the Icebox of the Nation.

1 ½ cups brown wild rice	1 (10¾-ounce) can
3 cups water	chicken broth
½ teaspoon salt	1 pound bacon,
¼ cup onion, chopped	fried and cut up
1 cup celery, chopped	½ pound ground beef,
1 teaspoon garlic salt	cooked and crumbled
1 tablespoon ground sage	3 cups Velveeta® cheese,
1 teaspoon salt	cubed
2 teaspoons pepper	1 pint half-and-half

Boil wild rice in water and ½ teaspoon salt until tender (about 1 hour), adding more water as needed. Add onion, celery, garlic salt, ground sage, salt, pepper, broth, bacon and ground beef. Simmer about 1 hour, adding more water as needed. Add cheese and half-and-half. Stir well over low heat until cheese is melted. Serve.

Yield: 12 to 15 servings

Cook's Note: This recipe can also be made in a slow cooker. Add rice, onion, celery, spices, broth and 3 cups of water to slow cooker, cook 6 to 8 hours on medium setting. Add remaining ingredients and continue to heat until cheese is melted.

Marge McClaren's Potato Salad

Verna Quaintance ◆ Pine County

Over the past 30 years Marge's potato salad has been served at many area graduations, weddings and family picnics. She began making it at her restaurant, Marge's Café, in Hinckley. It's been sold through Daggett's Super Valu in Hinckley since 1977.

2½ cups salad dressing
½ to 1 cup sugar
¼ to ½ cup evaporated milk
½ to 1 cup prepared mustard
5 pounds potatoes, boiled and diced
1 to 1½ cups celery, chopped fine
½ cup onion, chopped fine
2 to 2½ dozen eggs, boiled and chopped
salt and pepper to taste

Combine salad dressing, sugar, milk and mustard. Stir until smooth. In a large bowl combine potatoes, celery, onion and eggs. Add dressing mixture and mix to coat all. Add salt and pepper to taste. Refrigerate overnight. Be sure the dressing is sweet, as it will lose some sweetness after it sits. Don't make the dressing too runny.

Yield: 25 to 30 servings

Baked Northern

Richard Schmidt ◆ Mille Lacs County

8 (approximately) pounds fresh Northern Pike, whole and cleaned	½ cup celery, chopped
	½ cup onion, chopped
	½ cup fresh tomato, chopped
salt	1 teaspoon curry powder
½ cup butter	1 cup hot water
3 cups bread crumbs	

Place fish on aluminum foil on a large baking pan with sides. Salt both sides of fish. Melt butter in sauce pan and add bread crumbs, celery, onion, tomato, curry powder and hot water. Dressing should be moist enough to stick together, but not soggy. Stuff fish with dressing and tie with string. Score fish in 3 places, coat well with butter.

Bake uncovered at 400° until fish flakes easily (about 45 minutes).

Iron Miner's Pasties

Beatrice Ojakangas ◆ St. Louis County

This is a recipe our iron mining relatives regularly took to lunch. Iron miners in northern Minnesota and in the copper mines of the Upper Peninsula of Michigan carried pasties in their lunch pails everyday to the depths of the mines. The pasties were often baked fresh in the morning and wrapped so they would stay hot until lunchtime. The most commonly known pasties are simply filled with beef, potatoes, carrots and onions. In order to have a hot "dessert," some miners' wives baked an apple filling into one end of the pasty.

Pasties Dough:
    1 cup lard or shortening
    1 ¼ cups boiling water
    1 teaspoon salt
    4 ½ to 5 cups all-purpose flour

Beef-Vegetable Filling:
    1 pound top round of beef, cut into ½ inch pieces
    4 medium-sized potatoes, diced into ½ inch
    1 cup carrots, diced into ½ inch
    1 large onion, chopped
    1 teaspoon salt
    ½ teaspoon freshly ground black pepper

Apple Filling:
    4 medium-sized apples, pared, cored, sliced into 12 wedges each
    2 tablespoon sugar
    2 teaspoons flour
    ½ teaspoon ground cinnamon
    ⅛ teaspoon salt

Dough: In a large bowl, mix lard or shortening with boiling water and salt; stir until fat is melted. Add enough flour to make a stiff dough. Cover and refrigerate 1 hour or more. Divide into 8 parts. On a lightly floured board, roll out each part to make an oval, 11 inches long and 8 inches across. Preheat oven to 350°. Line 2 baking sheets with parchment paper or grease baking sheets.

Beef-Vegetable Filling: Combine the beef, potatoes, carrots, onions, salt and pepper.

Apple Filling: Mix the apples, sugar, flour, cinnamon and salt.

Put 1 cup meat mixture on center of each pastry oval, leaving enough space on 1 end of oval for the apple slices, and 2 to 2½ inches of margin along both sides of filling. Arrange 6 apples slices in a little pile on empty side of pastry oval, next to meat filling. Gently lift pastie edge up around meat and apple fillings. Pinch seam firmly lengthwise across top of pasty to make a seam about ½ inch wide and standing upright. Pinch with 2 fingers and thumb to make a pretty rope-like design. Repeat for each pastie. Place a wooden pick on end of pastie to mark apple end of filling. Arrange pasties on prepared baking sheets. Bake 1 hour or until golden. Serve hot or cooled to room temperature or refrigerate or freeze. Heat in a 300° oven before serving. Pasties are usually served with a pat of butter on top.

Yield: 8 pasties

Cook's Note: This makes an excellent picnic pie and a "meal in one." Today I serve pasties as a main course with a green salad.

Smoker Baked Beans

Mustang Steak House ◆ Kanabec County

2 (1-pound) bags of navy beans, cooked and drained	1 teaspoon salt
	1 teaspoon pepper
1 cup brown sugar, packed	garlic powder to taste
2 cups pulled pork	1 cup barbeque sauce
1 onion, chopped	2 cups ketchup
¼ cup molasses	

Put all ingredients together in a large pot. Cook 1 hour.

Yield: 1 gallon

Cook's Note: Serve these baked beans with ribs.

Nasi Goreng à la Nita

Nita Learmont ◆ Itasca County

I grew up in the Indonesian culture where the majority of the dishes contain hot chili peppers and exotic spices. My mother is well versed in this kind of cooking. She spent many hours a day preparing meals for her family. One of the dishes she made became my most favorite — Dendeng Balado (fried crispy beef with hot chili sauce.) When I moved away from my parents and started my own family, Dendeng Balado remained my favorite. One day, I was out of ideas for what to cook for breakfast. We had leftover Dendeng Balado, cooked rice and some homemade fresh pickles in the refrigerator. That's how Nasi Goreng à la Nita was born! This dish is easy to make, you can make it ahead of time, and most of the ingredients are available at the local grocery store.

Pickles (Acar):
1 large cucumber, peeled, seeded and cut into cubes
3 medium carrots, peeled and cut into cubes
1 Fresno red chili pepper, seeded and sliced
1 shallot, sliced
½ cup white vinegar
salt and sugar to taste

Fried Crispy Beef (Dendeng):
4 cups canola oil for frying
4 pounds beef sirloin steak, thinly sliced and lightly salted

Hot Chili Sauce (Sambalado):
¼ cup canola oil
1 whole garlic, diced
1 cup shallot, sliced
½ pound Fresno red chili peppers, seeded and sliced
1½ pounds ripe tomato, chopped
¼ cup Indonesian salty soy sauce
1 cup Indonesian sweet soy sauce
1 pound bag long grain rice, cooked
fried eggs
fried onions
leaf lettuce

Pickles: Mix all ingredients in a glass jar or a plastic container and refrigerate over night.

Fried Crispy Beef: Heat oil in a frying pan on medium. Fry the steak until crispy but not burned. (You might want to move the temperature to low setting when the steak is about half way done.) Drain on paper towel, set aside.

Hot Chili Sauce: Heat oil in a big wok or other big cooking pot. Fry garlic and shallots until fragrant. Add hot chili peppers, fry for 2 minutes and add tomatoes. Cook on low heat until most of the liquid evaporates. Pour in both salty and sweet soy sauce and stir. Pour the cooked rice into the hot chili sauce and stir until rice is all coated. Keep warm.

To serve: Fry the eggs to your liking, and wipe off excess oil. Put the chili sauce in the center of the plate; spread beef on the chili sauce, top with fried egg, and sprinkle with fried onions. Assemble lettuce leaves on one side of the plate, and put about two tablespoons of drained pickles on top.

Yield: 8 to 10 servings

Cook's Note: This can also be served buffet style, usually for breakfast, but also for lunch or dinner.

Yelena's Famous Russian Beef Stroganoff

Yelena Quistad ◆ Cook County

Here's the legend of this recipe: The name Beef Stroganoff (Boeuf à la Stroganoff) was named after Stroganov, a Russian count in the 1800s. He loved beef all his life, but became so old he couldn't chew his steaks. So he asked his creative cook to do something. The cook came up with the idea to cut beef into strips and cook it in sauce until tender.

I brought this recipe from Russia to Minnesota in 1995 and made some changes to make it easier to cook. During my cooking experience at Old Northwoods Lodge, a small resort on the Gunflint Trail, it was the most popular and desirable item on menu. I wanted to keep the recipe a secret and keep the tradition of a mysterious screen on everything coming from Russia. But now is the time for it to come out!

Beef Stroganoff:
2 pounds tenderloin part of beef, cut crosswise in strips
(½ to ⅓ x½-inch)
crushed black pepper to taste
kosher salt to taste, optional
1 small white or red onion, chopped or diced
1 tablespoon paprika (I use Hungarian, but smoked is fine), optional
⅛ teaspoon ground cloves, optional
2 tablespoons tomato paste or under 1 cup tomato juice
¼ cup fresh parsley, finely chopped

Sour Cream Sauce:
1 cup sour cream
1 to 1½ cups warm water
2 to 3 tablespoons flour
2 to 3 tablespoons cold water
2 to 3 tablespoons flour with equal water

Garnish:
scallions and parsley for garnish, finely cut

Beef Stroganoff: Trim tenderloin and cut into strips. Use a large frying pan with 2 inch sides. Heat frying pan on hot stove first (no butter or oil) and fry beef 5-10 minutes with salt and black pepper, until dark gold/light brown; in the beginning beef will stick to frying pan, but when beef reaches the right color it will be easy to stir. Add onion and keep cooking, stirring occasionally, until beef is fried equally and no liquid is left. Add paprika, ground cloves and tomato paste. If using tomato juice, cook until liquid is ½ gone, stirring occasionally. Remove frying pan from heat. It is important to take the pan away from the heat before you add the sour cream!

Sour Cream Sauce: Whisk sour cream and warm water together until smooth. Do not make it too thick – you need to be able to pour the sour cream as a liquid, but not too watery, as it is a base for your sauce – the more sauce the better! You can also use beef stock.

Slowly pour sauce into the frying pan with beef, and keep whisking the sour cream into the beef. Return frying pan to burner, on medium/low heat and continue to whisk and stir for 1 to 2 minutes or until the sauce starts to cook.

To thicken the sauce, mix 2 to 3 tablespoons of flour and an equal amount of water in a separate bowl and make it thick like pancake batter, and slowly add into the pan with beef stroganoff, on very low heat. Stir until sauce becomes smooth and thick. Add parsley and adjust salt, pepper and seasonings, keep cooking on small flame and let the sauce "puff" for a little while, but do not dry it out.

Yield: 8 servings

Cook's Note: Serve on noodles, mashed or pan-fried potatoes, cooked rice, polenta, orzo, buckwheat or kasha.

Pierogies

Marlene Wiczek ✦ Morrison County

My grandparents came from Poland, and my husband is Polish, too. Pierogies are a well-known Polish dish and can be made with a variety of fillings like fruit, meat or sauerkraut.

Pierogie Dough:
 4 cups flour
 2 eggs
 5 tablespoons sour cream
 6 tablespoons vegetable oil
 ¼ teaspoon salt
 ¾ cup water

Meat Filling (Miesem):
 1 pound (4 cups) pork, lamb, veal, or beef, cooked and ground
 2 tablespoons butter
 1 medium onion, chopped
 2 eggs, beaten
 ½ teaspoon salt
 ½ teaspoon pepper

Sauerkraut Filling (Pierogi z Kaputzy Kwaszone):
 1 pound sauerkraut
 2 tablespoons butter
 1 medium onion, chopped
 ¼ teaspoon salt
 ¼ teaspoon pepper

Blueberry Filling (Nadzienie z Czarnych Jagod):
 4 cups fresh blueberries
 3 teaspoon sugar

Vanilla-Cheese Filling (Pierogi Waniliowe):
 2 pounds (4 cups) dry cottage cheese or ricotta cheese
 1 egg yolk
 1 teaspoon vanilla extract
 ¼ cup seedless raisins
 ¼ teaspoon salt
 sugar to taste

Pierogi Dough: Sift flour into a large bowl; make a well in the center. Break eggs into well. Add sour cream, 3 tablespoons oil and salt. Blend ingredients with your finger tips, gradually adding water and kneading mixture into a smooth dough. Divide dough into quarters. Cover three portions with a damp cloth. On a lightly floured board, roll 1 dough portion into a rectangle about 1/16 of an inch thick. Cut into 3½-inch circles. In center of each dough circle, place 1 heaping tablespoon of meat, cheese, or fruit filling. Fold dough in half over filling and pinch to seal.

Bring a large saucepan of salted water to a boil, using ½ teaspoon salt per 2-quarts of water. Drop about 5 pierogies into boiling water. Stir gently so they don't stick to the bottom. When water returns to boil, add 5 more pierogies. Stir, then cover with a tight-fitting lid and cook over medium heat about 5 minutes or until they float. Gently remove pierogies from pot; drain in strainer and rinse with hot water. Repeat until all pierogies are boiled.

Meat Filling: Cook meat, remove from skillet. Melt butter in skillet, add onion and sauté until tender. Stir in meat and eggs. Sauté over medium heat for 5 minutes. Season with salt and pepper. Let cool. Makes enough to fill 40 to 45 pierogies.

Sauerkraut Filling: In a medium saucepan, place sauerkraut and enough water to cover; simmer uncovered over low heat for 30 minutes. Drain well. Use a food processor to process sauerkraut. Melt butter in large skillet. Add onion and sauté over medium heat until tender. Blend in sauerkraut, salt and pepper. Let cool. Makes enough to fill 40 to 45 pierogies.

Blueberry Filling: Wash berries and drain. In a medium bowl, sprinkle with sugar and mix lightly. Fill pierogie shells immediately before juice is drawn out of blueberries. Makes enough to fill 40 to 45 pierogies. Fruit-filled pierogies need to cook 10 to 15 minutes.

Vanilla-Cheese Filling: Process cheese in food processor (not too fine). In a large bowl, combine cheese, egg yolk, vanilla, raisins and salt. Add sugar to taste. Makes enough to fill 40 to 45 pierogies.

Yield: Makes about 70 pierogies

Cook's Note: Serve meat or sauerkraut pierogies with sautéed onions; fruit-filled or vanilla-cheese pierogies can be served with melted butter and softened cream cheese.

Croppas

Ann Meyer ◆ Cass County

My grandmother has been gone for almost 40 years, and this recipe of hers has been in my family for as long as I can remember. Last year, I received a box from my aunt that contained all my grandmother's recipe boxes and books, as well as hundreds of recipes she clipped from the newspaper. I was looking through one Slavonian cookbook, and there was our family favorite — croppas! When I try to explain to people what croppas are, a few eyebrows are raised. My kids beg me to make them for holidays.

Dough:
2½ cups flour
½ teaspoon salt
1 cup water, warm

Filling:
1 (16-ounces) container cottage cheese
½ teaspoon salt
½ teaspoon pepper
½ teaspoon garlic salt
2 eggs
4 slices of bread, torn into small pieces
butter, melted

Dough: Fill a Dutch oven half full of water and put on stove to boil. Mix flour, salt and warm water and knead until not sticky. Divide into 5 pieces, drop onto floured surface and roll each piece into 5 inch circles.

Filling: Mix filling ingredients together. Spread filling on dough, roll up and seal edges (if flour won't allow edges to seal, wet edge with a bit of water). Drop into boiling water carefully so they do not break. Boil 20 minutes. Drain. Cut up, and pour melted butter over them.

Yield: 5 servings

Cook's Note: Croppas are delicious with ham and coleslaw.

Apple Sauerkraut Country Pork

Mary and Marty Raddatz ◆ Todd County

Sunday was Dad's day in the kitchen, when he cooked and did dishes. Mom was given the day off. This was Dad's favorite meal to fix for Sunday dinner, which was right after church.

1 (4- to 5-pounds) boneless whole pork loin roast,
   cut into quarters
1 teaspoon garlic, minced
1 (27-ounce) can sauerkraut with juice
3 medium tart (Haralson) apples, sliced
1 large onion, chopped
1 cup apple juice
½ cup brown sugar, packed
½ teaspoon caraway seeds

Rub sides of roast with garlic. Place sauerkraut and half of the apples and onions in a 6-quart slow cooker. Top with pork roast. Warm the apple juice to dissolve brown sugar and pour over the pork. Sprinkle with caraway seeds and then cover with remaining apples and onions. Cover and cook on high for 4 to 5 hours or until a meat thermometer reads 160°.

Yield: 10 to 12 servings

Rabbit Stew with Dumplings
(Wabooz Naboob Ninawaa Napudin)

Kathy Peil ◆ Carlton County

When I was young, our family ate foods that were primarily "off the land." Venison, fish, rabbits, partridge and wild rice were especially common for winter meals. My mother was a dedicated hunter, and she thoroughly enjoyed providing meat for the family table. Many generations of Ojibwe people before her had done the same thing, so I guess it was culturally ingrained in her. Traditionally, that should have been a man's role, but my mother was a real tomboy. She spent a lot of time hunting with my uncles and could out-hunt them most of the time.

My mother would get four or five rabbits, then she would bake them in the oven, sometimes covering them with onions and make what she called "government gravy" to pour over them. It was delicious! Other times we had fried rabbit, similar to fried chicken, browned in a cast-iron frying pan, then baked in the oven.

Rabbit, or *wa-booz*, is traditional food for northern Minnesota Ojibwe. They are plentiful, tasty and relatively easy to hunt or trap, which is particularly important in this climate. Ojibwe people in days gone by had to do whatever they could to survive, and in the cold, it wasn't always easy to hunt bigger game like deer and moose. Fishing through the ice in sub-zero weather wasn't always practical, so a means to catch smaller game was developed – the snare.

A rabbit snare is a wire noose hung from a small, secure stick directly over a rabbit trail. When a rabbit runs through the noose, it's caught. Snares in days past were most likely made of tree roots or sinew instead of the picture wire we use now.

The foods the Ojibwe people ate were low in fat and primarily protein. Rabbit, venison and fish are very low in cholesterol. Wild rice is a complex carbohydrate that was eaten sparingly, because it had to last from season to season. Vitamin C was obtained from local berries and not tropical citrus fruit like we eat today.

Today, I still get a craving for the traditional foods I grew up on. So every winter, I try to find younger people who still hunt or snare rabbits.

These recipes are updated and, of course, use more modern techniques and ingredients. While preparing them, I think of my ancestors and their struggles to survive in our frigid weather, doing whatever they could to gather food, not having an electric stove or warm kitchen to cook it in. I am fortunate they did what they did so I can have the life I have today.

Stew:	**Dumplings:**
1 rabbit	2 cups flour
seasoned salt and pepper	1 teaspoon salt
½ cup onion, chopped	2 eggs, beaten
½ cup celery, chopped	water
½ stick butter	1 cup frozen peas
8 cups chicken broth	
2 cups carrots, chopped	
5 potatoes, peeled and cubed	

Stew: Sprinkle rabbit with seasoned salt and pepper and bake 2 hours at 350°. When done, let cool, and take the meat off the bones. Set meat aside in a bowl. Sauté onions and celery in butter and put in a large kettle. Add chicken broth and carrots and cook over medium heat for 10 minutes. When carrots are almost done, add potatoes and cook 15 minutes. After the potatoes are done add the rabbit.

Dumplings: Mix flour and salt with two beaten eggs; add enough water to make a stiff dough. Drop by teaspoonfuls into simmering stew. Let cook, uncovered, for 10 minutes. Add frozen peas as a final touch and let stand a few minutes to absorb.

Wild Rice Hotdish

Norma M. Hesse ◆ Aitkin County

1 cup wild rice	1 cup celery, chopped
2½ cups water	1 (10¾-ounce) can cream of
1 teaspoon salt	mushroom soup
1 pound ground beef	¾ cup water
¼ cup onion, chopped	

Rinse rice several times by placing in wire strainer, run cold water through it, lifting rice with fingers to clean thoroughly. Heat rice, water and salt to boiling, reduce heat. Cover and simmer until tender about 40 to 50 minutes. In frying pan brown the ground beef, onions and celery; add the can of soup with ¾ cup of water. Mix all together and put in casserole and bake for about 1 hour at 350°.

Yield: 5 to 6 servings

Cook's Note: Turn any leftovers into soup by adding 1 can of cream of mushroom soup and water.

Walleye Chowder

Debra Kellerman ◆ Lake of the Woods County

G reetings from the "Top of the Nation" – our slice of heaven known as the Northwest Angle and Islands. We're the most unique piece of real estate in Minnesota and the United States since we're attached to them only by water. Travelers must enter Canada to reach us via land. Since we're located on the premier walleye fishery in the state, we're proudly submitting the following recipe for the Sesquicentennial cookbook.

2 quarts potatoes, diced	2 cups chicken broth
1 cup carrots, diced	juice from ½ lemon
1 cup onions, chopped	½ stick butter
1 cup celery, chopped	¼ cup flour
2 bay leaves	1 pint whipping cream
7 cups water	salt and pepper to taste
2 pounds walleye fillet,	parsley flakes
cut into small chunks	

Combine potatoes, vegetables, bay leaves and 4 cups water in a 4-quart saucepan. Bring to a boil and simmer for 20 minutes uncovered. While vegetables are cooking, put fish and chicken broth in a 3-quart saucepan and bring to a boil. Simmer 10 minutes. Add lemon juice.

In a 6-quart pan or Dutch oven, melt butter; add flour stirring for 2 to 3 minutes. Add 3 cups water and bring to a boil. Add vegetables, fish and chicken broth to the large pan. Just before serving, add the cream and season with salt and pepper to taste. Heat just to boiling. Garnish with parsley flakes and serve.

Yield: 8 to 12 servings

Northern Minnesota Venison Meatballs

The Ebelings and The Wolters –
The "Longville" Cabin Owners ◆ Cass County

N orthern Minnesota is famous for its abundance of deer. This is a favorite appetizer with unique flavor. We submitted it in honor of our great friend and neighbor, Gary Dieckman, who is a true Minnesota outdoorsman, a logger, hunter and trapper.

1 pound ground venison	½ cup breadcrumbs
2 tablespoons onion, ground	⅔ cup milk
1 teaspoon salt	¼ cup flour
⅛ teaspoon pepper	2 tablespoons oil
⅛ teaspoon nutmeg	1 beef bouillon cube
⅛ teaspoon allspice	1 cup water
1 egg	

Mix together the venison, onion, salt, pepper, nutmeg, allspice, egg, bread-crumbs and milk. Roll into small balls and dredge in flour. Place 2 table-spoons of oil on a cookie sheet and place meatballs in a single layer. Bake at 350° for 30 minutes. Drain meatballs and place in slow cooker. Dissolve beef bouillon cube in 1 cup water and pour over meatballs. Serve warm.

Yield: 8 to 10 servings

Bannock

Bob Swanson ◆ Cook County

It would be nice to have some type of bread with a meal. If you happen to have access to flour, baking powder, sugar and grease here is a good recipe for Bannock, a North woods staple for many generations.

2 cups flour	2 tablespoons grease or
2 teaspoons baking powder	shortening
3 tablespoons sugar	1 cup to 1¼ cups milk
½ teaspoons salt	or water

Mix dry ingredients together. Cut in cold grease or shortening with fork or spatula. Add liquid and mix together until a dough forms. Place dough in a 10-inch oven proof skillet. Bake in a preheated oven at 425° for 25 to 30 minutes.

Cook's Note: You can cook this over coals or an open fire. Cook in a 10-inch skillet about 10 minutes or until sides of dough pull away from the sides of the pan. Flip the bread over if you care to in order to brown both sides. Another method is to use green (fresh) sticks. Use just 1 cup of milk or water. Form a handful of dough around a green stick and hold over coals until browned.

Yield: 6 to 8 servings

Ol' Ranger Chili

Ron Karels ◆ St. Louis County

I retired as manager of McCarthy Beach State Park in 2003.

1 pound ground beef
1 medium onion, chopped, coarse or fine, your choice
2½ cups water
1 stalk celery (works best if ya cut it up)
1 green pepper (again, it works best if ya cut it up)
3 shakes of hot pepper sauce
1 (4 ounce) can of mushrooms, juice and all
1 teaspoon black pepper
1 teaspoon mustard seed
1 teaspoon mustard powder
½ teaspoon minced garlic
1 (15 ounce) can of tomato sauce
¼ teaspoon peppercorns
¼ teaspoon onion powder
¼ teaspoon crushed red pepper
2 (15 ounce) cans kidney beans
2 shots Worcestershire sauce
1 teaspoon horseradish mustard (if you don't like this kind,
   you may substitute the sissy kind)
1 teaspoon horseradish
1 bay leaf
½ teaspoon chili powder
½ teaspoon cayenne powder
1 (6 ounce) can tomato paste
1 tablespoon red wine vinegar
2 tablespoons brown sugar
¼ teaspoon seasoned salt

Brown the ground beef in a large pot, and then add the remaining listed ingredients. Add that just-about-empty ketchup bottle left in the fridge. And if you have one lone carrot in the fridge, dice it up real small and toss it in, too. Add a snort of wine or cooking sherry, making sure all of the stuff lands in the pot. Not enough beans in the pot? No kidney beans? Nobody looking? Dump in a can of pork and beans. Then add one mystery ingredient, just for fun (your choice).

Mother's Rhubarb Crisp

Kay Favreau-Dickie ◆ Crow Wing County

Base:
4 cups rhubarb, cut
   into 1-inch pieces
1½ cups sugar
⅓ cup candied ginger,
   chopped
¾ cup flour

Crumb topping:
¾ cup flour
1 teaspoon cinnamon
½ cup brown sugar
1 cup cold butter
¾ cup oatmeal

whipped cream or ice cream

Base: Mix rhubarb, ¾ cup of the sugar and candied ginger and let soak for one hour. Mix together ¾ cup sugar and flour, add to rhubarb mixture and pour into buttered 9x13-inch oven dish.

Crumb topping: Combine topping ingredients and sprinkle over base. Bake in a preheated oven at 375° for 45 to 55 minutes until bubbles are clear. Serve warm with whipped cream or ice cream.

Yield: 10 to 12 servings

My Sister's Easy Easy Fudge

Heather Sletten ◆ Pine County

My sister came up with this recipe back in high school in the '80s. We make it all the time, especially for potlucks, classroom treats and anytime I need a quick sweet.

1 (12-ounce) package chocolate chips
1 tub ready-to-spread cake frosting

In microwave-safe bowl heat chocolate chips, stirring often until melted and smooth. Stir in frosting. Spread in buttered 12x12-inch pan or 8x8-inch pan. Cool in fridge until set then cut into small squares and eat!

Yield: 1 good-sized plate of fudge

Easy Sugar Cookies

Faythe Kinnunen ◆ Wadena County

I got this recipe more than 50 years ago, and the only directions said to roll the dough out and cut with a cookie cutter. To keep my grandchildren busy when they came to visit, one would measure the dry ingredients and work in the shortening with a pastry blender. Another would break and beat the eggs, measure sugar and vanilla and mix that all together. Flattening them was easier than using the rolling pin and cookie cutters. One of my grandsons came into the kitchen one day with two handfuls of cookies and said, "I don't like these cookies – I only eat them to keep Grandma happy!" For his next birthday he got a tin of these cookies!

3 cups flour	1 cup shortening
½ teaspoon baking powder	2 eggs, beaten
½ teaspoon baking soda	1 cup sugar
pinch of salt	1 teaspoon vanilla
pinch of nutmeg	

Mix flour, baking powder, baking soda, salt, nutmeg and shortening. In a separate bowl mix eggs, sugar and vanilla. Add egg mixture to flour mixture. Roll the dough into balls and flatten with bottom of a glass or cookie press. Place cookies on an ungreased cookie sheet and bake in a preheated oven at 350° for 12 minutes.

Yield: 4 to 5 dozen

Scotch Toffee

Ann and Richard Madsen ◆ Mille Lacs County

Minnesota is the Land of 10,000 Lakes, and the one I know best is Mille Lacs.

Between Isle and Wahkon there was a wonderful resort called Hazelglade. It was started and run by Hazel Lundsten, but later she married Frank Gudridge, and they ran it together. My family started going to Hazelglade in 1948 when I was three. We continued going there every summer until we bought our own property next door so we could build our own cabin but still enjoy Hazel and Frank.

Hazelglade was a wonderful family resort with about seven cabins and a lodge. Every one of the builidngs was decorated with Hazel's hand-painted rosemaling. I have many special memories of pumping water by hand, my dad taking us for rowboat rides, using the outhouse, lying in bed at night and watching my parents' shadows on the ceiling. (The walls didn't go all the way to the ceiling, so as my parents walked around, shadows were created by the kerosene lantern.) I remember Hazel's gorgeous roses (burying dead fish in the garden probably was beneficial), Frank bringing around huge blocks of ice for the ice box in our cabin, Gypsy, the black lab, befriending everyone, and lots of swimming.

The lodge – a grand place – had a big stone fireplace and a real bearskin rug! Every Sunday from Mother's Day through Labor Day, there was a smorgasbord at the lodge. Boy, was that a feast! I vividly recall being so full afterward that I could hardly walk back to the cabin. There were three tables in the smorgasbord – the hors d'oeuvres, the main entrées and the desserts. Hazelglade is where I was introduced to, and learned that I loved, pickled herring.

Hazelglade cabins became more modernized over the years. Hazel and Frank ran the resort for 44 years, and the smorgasbords remained a highlight.

2 cups oatmeal
½ teaspoon salt
⅓ cup shortening, melted
½ cup brown sugar, packed
¼ cup corn syrup
½ teaspoon vanilla
½ bag chocolate chips

Grease 9x13-inch pan. Mix together all ingredients except chips. Pat mixture in the pan. Bake at 400° for 10 to 12 minutes. Don't over cook it – just until it bubbles all over. Remove from oven. Let sit for a couple of minutes then sprinkle with chocolate chips. When they are melted, smooth out with a fork leaving the fork lines for effect. Cut with a table knife before chocolate sets.

Yield: 24 servings

Prize-Winning Streusel Blueberry Coffee Cake

Betty Brandt ◆ Itasca County

Our three children learned how to pick blueberries after we moved to northern Minnesota. We'd go to the University of Minnesota experiment station in Grand Rapids or to one of the local blueberry farmers to pick our own. We would pick and pick blueberries from early morning until we had picked a number of buckets. Now my four-year-old granddaughter has learned how to pick blueberries. She even got some in her bucket and not just her mouth. On one outing, she looked at her grandmother bending over a bush to pick berries and exclaimed, "What a big behind you have!" Her mother told her it wasn't nice to say those things. My granddaughter replied, "You told me I should never lie. And look, when I bend over, my behind is bigger, too."

Each of my children made this recipe for a 4-H food project at the county fair. Two received purple ribbons and one received a blue!

Batter:
1 ½ cups sugar
1 teaspoon vanilla
½ cup butter, softened
2 eggs
1 cup milk

3 cups flour
4 teaspoons baking powder
½ teaspoon salt
2 cups blueberries, fresh
   or frozen

Streusel Topping:
½ cup butter, softened
1 cup sugar

⅔ cup flour
1 teaspoon cinnamon

Batter: Blend sugar, vanilla, butter, eggs and milk. Add dry ingredients; blend. Gently fold in blueberries and spread into a greased 9x13-inch pan.

Topping: Blend butter and sugar; add flour and cinnamon. Sprinkle topping onto batter.

Bake in a preheated oven at 350° for about 50 minutes for fresh blueberries and at least 60 minutes if frozen blueberries are used.

Yield: 18 servings

Pfeffernuesse (Peppernuts)

Vern Lueth ✦ Beltrami County

This is an old cookie recipe that came to Minnesota from Germany about 150 years ago. We've always made it during the holidays. As a child I would put a peppernut in my milk to soak a bit. When it was about to sink, I would take it out with a spoon and eat it. Our parents dipped theirs in their coffee.

¾ cup vegetable shortening	4¼ cups flour
1 cup white sugar	1 teaspoon ground cloves
¼ cup brown sugar	1 teaspoon ground
1 egg	cinnamon
½ cup dark corn syrup	1 teaspoon ground black
½ cup molasses	pepper
1 teaspoon baking soda	½ teaspoon salt
1 tablespoon hot water	

Cream shortening and sugars, beat in egg. Add syrup and molasses; mix soda in hot water and add to mixture. Sift flour and spices; add to mixture and mix well. Chill thoroughly in covered container. Roll into ropes (about the size of your little finger), cut into approximately ½-inch lengths. Place on greased baking sheet and bake in a preheated oven at 375° to 385° for 8 to 10 minutes or until golden brown.

Yield: About 400 small cookies, depending on size of "rope" and length of cut

Momma Margie's Rhubarb Custard Pie

Adrienne Cahoon ✦ Crow Wing County

In the fast-paced 21st century, there is a "slow travel" movement to return to the qualities that were hallmarks of the 1950s by reconnecting to the earth and the people who make up a community. It's taking time to explore the back roads and learn about a region from the people who live there. In the August 2007 issue of *Midwest Living* magazine, the editor so wisely stated, "To know a community is to know its pie," because to find the best pie in town one must talk to the locals.

My B & B guests enjoy this pie made with eggs supplied by organically fed free-range chickens and rhubarb supplied by a local farmer in my weekly Community Supported Agriculture (CSA) basket to supplement my own garden's bounty. CSA is a "farm-to-table" concept of supporting local growers who use sustainable farming practices by purchasing a seasonal (late-spring through early-fall) membership in return for a weekly basket of typically organic vegetables, flowers, fruits, eggs, herbs, honey or other farm products.

The CSA concept, whose roots reach back 30 years to Japan, is called "teikei" in Japanese, which translates to "putting the farmer's face on food." The fun comes in anticipating what is going to be in the week's basket and in planning a menu around the contents. Two products I got in the first two CSA baskets of the spring were asparagus and a jar of homemade rhubarb jam. So, I made apple bran pancakes to spread with rhubarb jam and creamy asparagus potato soup.

1 (9-inch) double pie crust, unbaked	½ teaspoon nutmeg
4 cup fresh rhubarb, cut up	3 eggs, beaten
1¾ cups sugar	3 tablespoons milk
4 tablespoons flour	2 tablespoons butter

Preheat oven to 450°. Line a 9-inch pie plate with 1 crust. Put rhubarb in bottom of pie plate. Blend sugar, flour and nutmeg; add eggs and milk. Mix well. Pour mixture evenly over the rhubarb. Dot with butter. Cover with a "lattice top" pastry. Before putting in the oven, I like to place a metal "pie crust shield" or strips of aluminum foil over pie crust. Bake for 30 minutes; reduce heat to 350° and bake until rhubarb is tender. Cool before serving.

Yield: 6 to 8 servings

Ice Cream Sandwich Dessert

Betty Arndt ◆ Todd County

This dessert is always a hit! The part of this recipe that takes the longest is unwrapping the sandwiches.

> 19 ice cream sandwiches (or more depending on your tastes!)
> 1 (12-ounce) carton whipped topping
> 1 (11¾-ounce) jar hot fudge topping
> 1 cup salted peanuts

Cut 1 ice cream sandwich in half. Place 1 whole and ½ sandwich along short side of an ungreased 9x13-inch pan. Arrange 8 or more sandwiches in opposite directions in pan. Spread half of the whipped topping on top of sandwiches. Then layer hot fudge topping on top of whipped topping. Add peanuts and another layer of sandwiches and the rest of the whipped topping. Garnish with more peanuts and enjoy!

Yield: 15 to 20 servings

No-Bake Raspberry-Blackberry Pie

Andy Hoppe ◆ Morrison County

> 1 (9-inch) graham cracker crust
> 1 cup sugar
> 1 cup crushed raspberries
> ⅔ cup water
>
> 3 tablespoons cornstarch
> ⅓ cup water
> 1 pint whole blackberries
> whipped cream, optional

Mix sugar, crushed raspberries and ⅔ cup water in skillet on medium heat until it boils. Add a small amount of the mixture to cornstarch and ⅓ cup water. Mix together until smooth. Add this mixture to the berry mixture and cook until thickened. Spread a small amount of raspberry mixture on the crust. Cool slightly. Place blackberries in crust. Pour remaining raspberry mixture over the blackberries, filling pie. Cool. Top with whipped cream if you choose.

Yield: 6 to 8 servings

Good and Easy Creamed Apple Pie

Cherry Brouwer ◆ Beltrami County

T his pie is so simple and always gets raves!

1 cup sugar	4 cups apples, diced
4 tablespoons flour	(2 to 3 Red Rome apples)
dash of salt	cinnamon
1 cup heavy cream	unbaked pie shell

Preheat oven to 425°. Mix sugar, flour and salt together. Add heavy cream. Place diced apples in unbaked pie shell. Spread cream mixture over apples and sprinkle with cinnamon. Bake for 12 to 15 minutes at 425° then 350° for 30 to 35 minutes.

Yield: 6 to 8 servings

Zucchini Pie

Rosalie Paul ◆ Itasca County

4 cups zucchini, peeled and cut up
½ cup brown sugar, packed
½ cup sugar
¼ teaspoon nutmeg
¼ teaspoon cinnamon
¼ teaspoon salt
3 tablespoons flour
2 tablespoons lemon juice
butter

Cover zucchini pieces with boiling water for 5 minutes, then drain. Mix sugars, nutmeg, cinnamon, salt, flour and lemon juice, add zucchini. Pour into pie tin, dot with butter. Bake in a preheated oven at 400° for 15 minutes, reduce temperature to 350° and bake another 45 minutes to an hour.

Yield: 6 to 8 servings

CENTRAL REGION

Since before statehood, the cities that grew into Minneapolis and St. Paul and the region surrounding them have been a hub for new immigrants. They bring with them the flavors and foods of home: soups from Ireland and Vietnam, curry from Thailand, kringla from Sweden, albondigas from Mexico. But like the immigrants themselves, those flavors and foods have blended into the community— Latin-American spices perking up butternut squash, lingonberries glaze bison tenderloin and home-grown veggies are chopped into salsa.

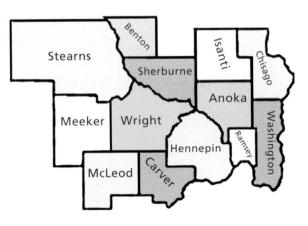

Oriental Chicken Wings

Cathy Carroll ✦ Carver County

1 cup sugar	1 cup soy sauce
1 cup water	1 teaspoon ginger
¼ cup pineapple juice	3 to 4 pounds chicken wings
½ cup corn oil	

In a large bowl dissolve sugar in water; add juice, corn oil, soy sauce and ginger; stir. Clean chicken wings and put in large zippered plastic bag. Add marinade to wings and refrigerate overnight. Bake at 300° for 2 hours. Remove wings from marinade and bake at 350° for 1 hour. Watch so they don't burn.

Yield: 6 to 8 servings

Farmer's Market Pineapple Salsa

Alex Wennberg ✦ Ramsey County

This recipe incorporates fresh, organic foods that are both delicious and healthy. Most of them can be bought at the St. Paul or Minneapolis Farmers' Markets. My family generally eats it on fish tacos – especially fish tacos made with perch caught in Minnesota's northern lakes.

1 cup pineapple, chopped	2 jalapeños, chopped
½ cup red bell pepper, diced	⅛ cup orange juice
½ cup green bell pepper, diced	⅛ cup lemonade
	¼ cup cilantro, chopped
1 cup corn kernels	½ teaspoon ground cumin
1 (15-ounce) can black beans	salt and pepper to taste
¼ cup onions, chopped	fresh lime for garnish

In a bowl, toss together all ingredients and flavor with salt and pepper. Garnish with fresh lime. Cover and chill until served.

Yield: These quantities serve 8, but are easily altered to serve fewer or more people.

Cook's Note: Although the salsa can be served with chips, it can also accompany chicken. Keeps well in the refrigerator for a few days.

Baked Spinach Artichoke Dip

Sara Johnson ◆ Wright County

1 (10-ounce) package frozen chopped spinach, thawed
1 (14-ounce) can artichoke hearts, drained
½ cup Parmesan cheese, grated
1 cup mozzarella cheese, shredded
¼ teaspoon white pepper, ground
1 teaspoon lemon juice
¼ cup Parmesan cheese, grated

Preheat oven to 350°. In a medium bowl, combine spinach, artichoke, ½ cup Parmesan, mozzarella, white pepper and lemon juice. Mix well and spoon into 1-quart baking dish. Top with ¼ cup Parmesan cheese. Bake for 15 to 20 minutes, or until hot and bubbly.

Yield: 4 to 6 servings

Dandelion Greens

Isabelle Schmidt ◆ Stearns County

My mother, Martha Schmidt, was born in 1913, and she remembers her mother, Sebella, using this recipe. This salad was made in the spring before other salad vegetables were available from the garden. In those days, salad greens weren't purchased in stores like they are today. Mother would tell how they were hungry for greens after going the winter without fresh vegetables.

bacon strips, enough to make 3 tablespoons bacon fat
2 teaspoon vinegar or fresh squeezed lemon juice
4 cups young spring dandelion leaves, washed and patted dry
salt and pepper to taste

Cut bacon strips into bits and fry. Mix vinegar or lemon juice to bacon bits and bacon fat. Pour mixture over the washed spring dandelions leaves. Add salt and pepper to taste.

Yield: 4 servings

Baked Swedish Pancake

Rose Paulson ✦ Washington County

My mother-in-law, Elsie Paulson, served this recipe on special occasions. It puffs up and then falls as you take it out of the oven. It's wonderful for breakfast, lunch or dinner.

> 4 slices bacon, fried and cut into small pieces
> 4 eggs
> 1 cup flour
> 2 cups milk
> 1 teaspoon salt
> 2 to 3 tablespoons reserved bacon drippings
> butter
> syrup

Fry bacon; drain, reserving 2 to 3 tablespoons bacon drippings. Pour the reserved bacon drippings into a 9x13-inch pan, coating bottom and sides. Add bacon pieces to pan. Beat the eggs well, add flour and milk alternately; add salt. Pour mixture over bacon pieces and bake at 375° for 30 to 40 minutes. Serve hot with butter and syrup.

Yield: 9 to 12 servings

Cook's Note: Serve with applesauce, sausages and/or bacon.

Swedish Pancakes

First Lady Mary Pawlenty ✦ Ramsey County

This is a special recipe I originally received many years ago from my oldest sister, Barbara. The original, a now gently aged recipe card, is a keepsake for me. I make these pancakes as often as I have time, and my family loves them. If serving a big family, be prepared to double or triple the recipe. These pancakes go fast!

4 eggs	½ teaspoon vanilla
1 cup milk	2 tablespoons sugar
2 tablespoons oil	1 cup flour (or slightly less)

In a medium bowl, beat together eggs, milk, oil, vanilla and sugar. Add flour and continue beating. Batter will be thin. Spoon batter onto a hot griddle or skillet that's been lightly oiled. As bubbles begin to form on surface, flip pancakes. It works best to use 2 pancake turners — 1 to lift the edge, the other to slide under the pancake and flip. Serve with the traditional lingonberry sauce, or our family's favorite — real butter and warm maple syrup.

Yield: 4 servings

Bouja

Donna Schafer ◆ Benton County

B ouja is a traditional dish served in this community of German and Polish settlers. This is perfect for a large gathering.

15 to 20 chickens	2 dozen bunches celery
125 pounds ox tails	1 bushel carrots
10 pounds lamb stew meat	1 bushel onions
1 bushel potatoes	4 gallons canned peas
2 bushels tomatoes or	4 boxes of soup barley
canned tomatoes	salt and pepper to taste
1 bushel cabbage	

Fill 2 bouja kettles ⅔ full of water; bring to boil, add all the raw meat. Boil about 3 hours. Add the vegetables one at a time. Add salt and pepper and more spices as desired. You may need to add more hot water during cooking. Stir constantly after vegetables are added. Remove the bones before serving. Takes approximately 6 hours.

Yield: 120 gallons

Cook's Note: Serve it with crackers and bars and cookies, of course.

Berry Good Breakfast Bake

Rep. Diane Loeffler - Minnesota Sesquicentennial
Commission member ◆ Hennepin County

I developed this recipe for the Holland Neighborhood Hotdish Revolution cooking contest and community fundraiser. Hotdish is a Minnesota tradition and served not just at home, but regularly at funeral lunches, fundraisers, post-game gatherings and whenever large groups gather. This recipe won both the 2006 Breakfast Bake and Best Name division and received, as a trophy, a vintage plate festooned with the details of the award noted in labeler tape.

Minnesota's history has been shaped by volunteer groups fueled by home-cooked food. The annual Hotdish Revolution is just one example of the thousands of community fundraisers held each year in all parts of Minnesota to fund park teams and school programs.

pie crust dough (store bought is fine – rolled or folded,
  not in the pan, or make your own)
1 (8-ounce) package light cream cheese, softened
1 (12-ounce) can whole cranberry sauce
1 cup strawberries, sliced
¼ teaspoon cinnamon

Preheat oven to 375°. Decide if you want lots of servings and a thin layer of fruit (use 9x13-inch pan) or fewer servings and a thicker layer of fruit (11x7-inch pan). Roll (or unfold) crust and place in pan. Trim with a sharp knife so that the crust just lines the bottom, not the sides. Save the trimmings carefully – they'll be used later.

Spread softened cream cheese over the crust using the back of a spoon. In a bowl mix the cranberry sauce, berries and cinnamon. Spread berry mixture over the cream cheese.

Now it's time to have fun. Using a sharp knife or cookie cutters, create a visually pleasing top for the fruit using the trimmed pie crust (for example, gingerbread figures, little houses, stars or stripes). You'll be accenting the fruit, most of which won't be covered. Bake at 375° until the top crust is browned (check at 35 minutes and then decide if more time is needed). Warm from the oven is my favorite, but it's also good cold.

Yield: Serves 8 to 20 depending on size of pan and size of serving

Chicken Dumpling Soup

Lori Larson ◆ Sherburne County

This soup is a meal in itself and perfect served on a cold winter day. The whole grains, boneless, skinless chicken breast and skim milk help make it healthier and keep it low in fat.

Chicken:

14 cups water	½ teaspoon turmeric
2 pound boneless, skinless	(added for color)
chicken breasts, thawed	1 teaspoon thyme
3 ribs celery, chopped	1 teaspoon black pepper
4 large carrots, peeled	½ teaspoon allspice
and diced	½ pound green beans, frozen
¼ cup onion, minced	and cut into small chunks
2 cups skim milk	½ cup brown rice
¼ cup chicken base	

Dumplings:

4 whole eggs	2 teaspoons salt
1 cup skim milk	¼ teaspoon black pepper
3 cups flour	2 tablespoons dried parsley
1 cup whole wheat flour	1 teaspoon baking powder
1 tablespoon wheat germ	

Chicken: Measure water into a 6-quart stock pot. Bring water to a boil. Add chicken breasts, celery, carrots and onion. Reduce heat and simmer 1 hour.

After chicken breasts have been cooked, remove them from the stock pot onto a cutting board. Allow to set until cool enough to handle. While chicken is cooling add milk, chicken base, seasonings, green beans and rice to the stock pot. Increase heat and allow soup to return to a boil. Dice the chicken breasts and add them to the soup. Reduce heat to a soft boil. Drop dumpling batter into soup ½ tablespoon at a time. Continue to cook for 20 minutes. Soup is now ready to serve.

Dumplings: While chicken is cooking, prepare the dumplings. Begin by placing the eggs and milk into a 2-quart mixing bowl. Mix thoroughly. In a separate bowl, combine the remaining dumpling ingredients. Add these dry ingredients to the egg mixture. Mix until blended. Set aside until ready to drop into soup.

Yield: 8 to 10 servings

Pork Hock Soup

Shirley Erickson ◆ Wright County

My in-laws, Bill and Lois Erickson of Cokato, gave this recipe to me after I married my husband, John. It uses everything available through the winter months. It's the best soup when it gets cold! The longer this soup simmers before serving, the better. Heating it up the next day is even better.

> 2 tablespoons whole allspice
> 1 pork hock, depending how big a batch you want to make, maybe 2 or 3, if desired
> 1 tablespoon salt
> 2 medium rutabagas, diced
> 6 large potatoes, cut into small chunks
> 3 to 5 large carrots, diced

Combine allspice and pork hock in large pot with water and salt, enough to cover pork hock. Bring water to a boil and simmer for at least 2 hours. Add rutabagas, potatoes and carrots; cover and simmer until vegetables are tender.

Yield: 1 large stockpot

The Gausman/Janecek Traditional Christmas Eve Oyster Stew

Sarah Janecek - Minnesota Sesquicentennial Commission member ◆ Ramsey County

One of the recipe treasures my mother, Jeanette Gausman, brought to her marriage in 1956 to my father, James Janecek – and then to our entire family in the ensuing 50-plus years – was this recipe for oyster stew. It was served in the farmhouse where my mother grew up, just outside Alberta, in the 1940s and '50s.

Decades later, growing up in suburban New Brighton, I read – rather, devoured – the complete Laura Ingalls Wilder *Little House on the Prairie* series of books at least three times. I loved those books (but loathed the television series).

One of the most memorable chapters was about the stark Christmas in *The Long Winter*. The Ingalls family had moved from the farm, where they lived in a sod house, into Pa's store building on Main Street to survive the winter. No trains had made it through the blizzards for weeks. There were no gifts in the store and no money to buy gifts, so the Ingalls family made simple gifts for each other from household scraps. The only Christmas splurge the family could afford was two small tins of oysters for Christmas dinner. Ma made a weak oyster stew from the last milk from Ellen, the cow, using the last of the coal to fire the stove. The rest of the winter the whole family braided straw to fuel the stove.

Every Christmas Eve, during the prayer or just after, we collectively pause to think about those family members who are no longer at our Christmas Eve table. Privately, I also think about all the Pas and Mas and Lauras in my family and others who came across the prairie before us. How grateful they were for two small tins of oysters and their Ellens. How the simple ingredients in the stew are basically the same as they've always been, except that the bowl before me is a sea of rich milk and butter swimming with fresh oysters, not those from a can.

The bounty we enjoy today could never have been fathomed by those Minnesotans who settled our state in the 19th century. But after I'm done thinking about them, I move on to what I'm quite sure they would want for me today. I slurp my stew and enjoy every last drop in the bowl. Then I ask, "Please, Ma, may I have another?"

2 quarts whole milk
1 pint cream
1 teaspoon salt
½ teaspoon white pepper
½ cup butter (1 stick)
5 pints oysters
oyster crackers
fresh pepper and salt to taste

In a large stockpot, heat (but do not boil) milk, cream, salt, white pepper and butter. In a separate kettle, heat the oysters until their edges curl. Add the oysters to the milk mixture and serve with oyster crackers. Pass the pepper mill and more salt!

Yield: Serves 6 to 8 oyster lovers

Pho Beef Soup

Van-Anh Hoang ✦ Ramsey County

Pho is a traditional Vietnamese noodle dish served in a bowl of broth.

Broth:
  1½ gallons of water
  5 pounds beef knee bones
  1 pound beef shank (remove after cooked for 2 hours)
  1 large onion
  1 chunk of ginger (size of your thumb)
  1 bag of "Pho spice" beef soup base (five star, clove, cinnamon, cilantro seed)
  2 teaspoons salt
  1 teaspoon sugar
  1 teaspoon black pepper
  1 teaspoon MSG (or a beef bouillon cube)
  2 carrots, optional
  1 white beet root, optional

Bowl:
  1 pound rice noodles
  1 bunch green onions, chopped
  1 small onion, very thinly sliced
  1 lemon, cut into 6 pieces
  1 small bunch cilantro, chopped
  1 pound raw beef steak, very thinly sliced across grain beef shank (removed from above broth after two hours), thinly sliced

Broth: Cook the beef bones, water and all broth ingredients listed above for 6 hours. Skim the fat and remove bones, vegetables and spices. Strain broth through fine strainer for a clear soup broth. Return broth to heat and bring to a rolling boil. Broth must be boiling hot when poured over bowl ingredients.

To serve: Cook rice noodles in boiling water for 1-2 minutes. Rinse with cool water and drain completely. Divide the noodles equally into 6 big bowls. Divide all remaining bowl ingredients equally into the 6 big bowls with the noodles. Pour the boiling broth into the bowls (over bowl ingredients) and serve immediately.

Note: Remove the beef shank after the first 2 hours of broth cooking time. Use the meat in the bowl ingredients.

Yield: 6 servings

Baked German Potato Salad

Larry and Jeanette Hoof ◆ McLeod County

1 cup bacon, diced, cooked and drained
8 cups potatoes, cooked and sliced
1 cup celery, diced
1 cup onion, chopped
3 teaspoons salt
3 teaspoons flour
⅔ cup sugar
⅔ cup vinegar
½ teaspoon pepper
1⅓ cups water

Fry bacon, drain drippings and return 4 tablespoons bacon grease to skillet. Place potatoes and bacon in a 3-quart baking dish. Add celery, onions, salt and flour to bacon grease. Cook gently. Add sugar, vinegar, pepper and water. Bring to a boil. Pour over potatoes and bacon in 3-quart baking dish. Cover and bake for 30 minutes at 350°.

Yield: Serves 12

Chicken Salad in Cheddar Pastry Cups

Patricia Miller ◆ Hennepin County

M any years ago, a friend and I went to England and fell in love with afternoon tea. When we got home, we took a "tea" class, and then wowed a little group of friends with a formal tea party. Since then, I've hosted dozens of tea parties for the holidays, for fundraisers and just for fun. I've put together a file of tea-party favorites, and this one always gets gobbled up.

Chicken Salad:
  8 ounces cooked chicken, cut up
  ¼ cup celery, finely chopped
  1 hard-cooked egg, finely chopped
  2 tablespoons sweet pickle relish, well drained
  salt and pepper to taste
  ¼ cup mayonnaise
  ¼ cup sour cream

Pastry Cups:
  ½ cup unsalted butter, softened
  1 cup sharp Cheddar cheese, grated
  1 ¼ cups flour
  dash each of pepper and seasoned or regular salt
  few drops of bottled hot pepper sauce
  fresh chives for garnish

Chicken Salad: In a medium bowl, combine all ingredients except mayonnaise and sour cream. In a small bowl blend mayonnaise and sour cream, and then fold into chicken mixture until well mixed. Cover and refrigerate.

Pastry Cups: Preheat oven to 350°. In a medium bowl, mix butter and cheese until well blended. Gradually stir in remaining ingredients except chives. Mix until dough is blended and clings together. Divide dough into 24 equal portions and roll each portion into a ball. Press each ball into a miniature muffin pan cup, working the dough up the sides. With a fork, prick the sides and bottoms of the shells. Cover and refrigerate 1 hour. Bake shells for 20 to 25 minutes until lightly browned. Pastry will begin to puff up in the cups, so after 10 minutes, reprick them. Cool slightly in the pan. Carefully lift the cups out – they're fragile. To serve, spoon about 1 tablespoon chicken salad into each cup and garnish with fresh chives.

Yield: 24 salad-filled cups

Cook's Note: These make a delicious luncheon or shower entrée, too. Just use regular-sized muffin pans. The recipe then makes 12. The shells also can be filled with your favorite salad.

Latin-Spiced Butternut Squash

Ann Sessoms ✦ Hennepin County

1 tablespoon cumin seeds
2 teaspoons whole black peppercorns
1 teaspoon coriander seeds
1½ teaspoons sugar
½ teaspoon kosher salt
¼ teaspoon cayenne pepper
4 pounds butternut squash, peeled, seeded and
    cut into 1-inch cubes
⅓ cup vegetable oil

Combine cumin, peppercorns and coriander in heavy, small skillet. Stir over medium heat until fragrant and toasted, about 8 minutes. Cool slightly. Finely grind toasted spices. Transfer to bowl. Add sugar, salt and cayenne pepper. Toss spice mix and remaining ingredients in large bowl to coat. Arrange squash on large rimmed baking sheet. Bake at 400° until squash is tender and beginning to brown, about 45 minutes, stirring occasionally.

Yield: 10 to 12 servings

County Clare's Irish Root Soup

Patti Lee Gates ◆ Anoka County

This soup truly is Irish soul food! Some of the vegetables in this recipe have been grown in Anoka County for years. It's a harvest in a bowl.

2 pounds sweet potatoes, peeled, halved,
   boiled and oven-roasted *
2 tablespoons olive oil
1 tablespoon butter
2 pounds carrots, peeled and sliced
2 leeks (white part only) sliced
6 cloves garlic, peeled and chopped
4 cups chicken stock
2 cups whipping cream plus whipped cream
   for garnish (or half-and-half)
pinch of salt
pinch of white pepper
2 tablespoons sugar or 1 tablespoon grated fresh ginger

* Boil potatoes about 10 minutes, then oven-roast by placing potatoes on cookie sheet in a preheated oven at 350° for about 30 minutes, or until browned and tender.

Heat oil and butter in large, heavy saucepan over medium heat. Add carrots, leeks, garlic and sweet potatoes. Sauté until leeks are translucent, about 8 minutes. Add stock and cream. Cover and simmer until carrots and potatoes are very soft, stirring occasionally, about 30 minutes.

Purée soup in batches in blender. Return soup to same saucepan. Add salt, pepper and sugar or fresh ginger. Taste and adjust seasonings. Stir soup over medium heat until heated through. Ladle into bowls and top with whipped cream.

Yield: 6 servings

Cook's Note: Use sugar for a slightly sweeter taste or add about 1 tablespoon grated fresh ginger to the veggies for a spicier flavor. Enjoy this soup hot or cold, for lunch or dinner, with a sandwich or a salad.

Delicious Salad with Poppy Seed Dressing

Pat Edlund ◆ Washington County

Each time there is a gathering, I receive a request to provide this refreshing salad.

Salad:
   1 (10- to 16-ounce) bag baby spinach
   1 bunch Romaine salad greens, torn into bite-size pieces
   3 red Fuji apples, diced with skin on
   1 (6-ounce) package dried craisins
   ½ cup sunflower seeds or cashews
   4 ounces mozzarella cheese, shredded

Dressing:
   ¾ cup sugar
   1 teaspoon dry mustard
   1 teaspoon salt
   1½ tablespoons onion, finely grated
   ⅓ cup cider vinegar
   1 cup canola oil
   1 tablespoon poppy seeds

Salad: Mix spinach and romaine lettuce. Add apples, craisins, sunflower seeds and cheese into a large bowl.

Dressing: Mix dressing ingredients in a jar and shake well. Refrigerate and pour over salad just before serving.

Yield: 12 servings

Sauerkraut Pie

Karen Lueck Covington ◆ McLeod County

This recipe celebrates the heritage of the many people who came from Germany to Minnesota in the 1800s. The apples in it are a different twist — a change from the expected taste.

> 1 cup pork, cooked and shredded
> 1 cup sauerkraut
> 1 cup beef broth
> ¼ teaspoon pepper
> 3 apples, diced and cooked in microwave until tender
> 2 cups potatoes, mashed
> 1 tablespoon butter

Mix pork, sauerkraut, broth, pepper, and apple. Put into greased 1½-quart baking dish. Cover with mashed potatoes. Dot with butter. Bake at 350° until top is brown, about 30 minutes.

Yield: Serves 6

Pork Chops à l'Orange

Kurt J. R. Swenson ◆ Chisago County

When I was in 4-H, this was one of my entries in the Foods Revue. Our family raised hogs so we had pork chops on a regular basis.

> 6 (½-inch thick) pork chops
> ½ teaspoon seasoned salt
> 1 large onion, sliced
> 1 (6-ounce) can of orange juice concentrate
> ¼ cup brown sugar, packed
> ¾ cup of water
> 3 tablespoons lemon juice
> ½ teaspoon allspice

Brown both sides of pork chop on medium heat in greased electric skillet, drain. Sprinkle with seasoned salt. Place sliced onions on top of chops. Combine remaining ingredients and pour over chops. Bring to boil, reduce heat and simmer for 25 minutes or until tender.

Yield: 6 pork chops

Cook's Note: This recipe is great for venison chops, too. These pork chops are tasty served with fresh boiled parsleyed red potatoes, garden-fresh steamed green beans, dinner rolls and your favorite dessert.

Grandmother's Homemade Sauerkraut

Karen Lueck Covington ◆ McLeod County

For my mother, my maternal grandmother and great-grandmother, cooking and baking were not an exact science achieved with measuring cups and measuring spoons. It was a skill that came from experience and experimenting. They developed a talent for eyeing proportions and knowing what amount looked just right. They could add a dash of this or a pinch of that, and somehow, their food preparation was always a success.

My great-grandparents on both sides of the family came from Germany. I tease my children that this ties our family line to sauerkraut. It's also nutritious – sauerkraut is rich in vitamins C and K.

My grandmother made homemade sauerkraut. As I grew up in the 1940s and 1950s, our family would have fried sauerkraut, which was fried along with the meat prepared for the meal. It was an accompaniment to pork – like mushrooms with steak. Sauerkraut was served as a vegetable and in main dishes like my mother's recipe for pork hocks and my sauerkraut pie recipe. My daughter now makes sauerkraut hotdish – a favorite in her home.

> cabbage, shredded
> coarse salt

Shred enough cabbage to fill a crock, throw in a handful of coarse salt, mixing the salt into the cabbage. Cover the cabbage with a plate (placed upside down), and set a rock on top to apply pressure to the fermenting cabbage. As the cabbage ferments, dip off rising liquid. It should be done fermenting and ready to can in 14 days.

Yield: 1 crock

Trini's Albondigas

Conrad and Christine Pena ◆ Ramsey County

This recipe was a favorite of Augustine and Trinidad Garcia's family. The two met in St. Paul shortly after arriving separately from Mexico, making them among the first Mexicans to settle on the West Side. According to family members, Trini would make a large pot of her albondigas and kept it on the stove all afternoon for anyone who happened to come by to enjoy. On Sundays, this meant the whole family — children, spouses and grandchildren — spent time in the kitchen eating albondigas with fresh tortillas.

This recipe comes from the *Bend in the River...A Place on the Hearth Recipes* cookbook from the West Side Safe Neighborhood Council, 1988.

2 pounds ground beef
1 cup raw rice
1 small egg
1 cup tomato sauce
3 medium potatoes, cut into 1 inch cubes
3 carrots, cut into rings
garlic to taste
salt to taste
1 tablespoon of Lieva Buena (mint leaves), dry

Fill an 8-quart kettle ¾ full with water; bring to a rolling boil. In a large bowl, mix ground beef, raw rice and egg. Make into meatballs the size of golf balls and place into the boiling water. Note that the water in the kettle must be at a rolling boil before putting in the meatballs or the meatballs will not become firm. Add the tomato sauce, potatoes and carrots. Season with garlic and salt to taste. Add mint leaves. Simmer for 45 to 60 minutes, covered. When a film develops on the surface of the water, skim it off.

Yield: 6 servings

Hungarian Cabbage

Alice Robinson ◆ Stearns County

This recipe is one of my favorites from my mother who was an excellent cook. She was of Polish descent, so we enjoyed many ethnic dishes prepared by her and her sisters. This is a wonderful ethnic Hungarian side dish that goes well with anything and is good to take to potlucks.

5 slices bacon, diced	3 cups egg noodles, cooked
2 teaspoon sugar	1 cup sour cream
1 teaspoon salt	paprika
6 cups cabbage, chopped	

Sauté bacon until crisp. Stir sugar and salt into bacon drippings. Add cabbage, stirring until coated with drippings. Cover and simmer 7 to 10 minutes. Add cooked noodles and bacon. Stir to mix. Spoon into a 2-quart casserole. Cover and bake at 325° for 45 minutes. Remove from oven and spread sour cream over top. Sprinkle with paprika and bake 10 minutes longer.

Yield: 8 servings

Reuben Pizza

Nicole German ◆ McLeod County

This recipe was a runner-up in Quick Cooking magazine's Pizza Pleasers recipe contest. We have it on pizza night, which is usually Friday.

1 (12-inch) pre-made pizza crust
Thousand Island or Russian salad dressing
½ pound deli corned beef, beef, pork or ham, thinly sliced and cut into ¼-inch strips
sauerkraut, drained
Swiss cheese, shredded

Top pizza crust with dressing, followed by meat, sauerkraut and cheese. Bake in a preheated oven at 350° for 10 to 15 minutes or until cheese is melted.

Yield: 4 to 6 servings

Greek Shrimp

Greg Lauer ◆ Ramsey County

This recipe was given to my wife and me as part of our wedding cookbook. It's a dish we have made many times over the years. My family likes to make it in summer when the garden is overflowing with tomatoes.

Skillet 1:
    2 tablespoons olive oil
    1 teaspoon garlic, diced
    2 cups tomatoes, peeled and cubed
    ½ cup dry white wine
    salt and pepper to taste
    ¼ cup fresh basil, diced
    1 teaspoon dried oregano

Skillet 2:
    3 tablespoons olive oil
    1 ½ pounds shrimp
    ⅛ teaspoon red pepper

    8 ounces feta cheese
    pasta, cooked

In skillet 1: Heat 2 tablespoons oil. Add garlic and tomatoes. 1 minute later add wine. Add herbs and simmer for approximately 10 minutes.

In skillet 2: Heat 3 tablespoons oil. Add shrimp and sprinkle with red pepper. Cook until shrimp are tender.

Preheat oven to 400°. In baking dish, pour shrimp mixture into baking dish. Then pour tomato mixture into baking dish. Crumble and sprinkle feta cheese over top. Bake 10 minutes. Serve over pasta.

Yield: 4 to 6 servings

Cook's Note: We serve it on farfalle pasta and usually pair it with salad and a baguette.

Pickled Fish

Shirley Welch ◆ Wright County

For more than 80 of the years that Minnesota has been a state, three generations of my family have fished the lakes of Wright County. During 20 summers, people living on Lake John could set their clocks according to my husband's trolling journey. Leaving our door each morning, he began the search for a "great northern," just the perfect size. As a true conservationist, he practiced catch-and-release to make sure large fish lived to reproduce and the smaller ones could grow up.

He perfected a cleaning technique that removed all the bones that cause many people to shun this very delicious fish. A taste test conducted by locals upheld our belief when they chose the northern pike as the "preferred" fish.

This recipe for pickled fish provided a favorite appetizer for guests at our summer home.

> 2½ pounds raw northern fillets
> 1½ cups pickling salt
> 1 gallon water
> white vinegar (various amounts)
> 3 cups sugar
> pickling spice (1 teaspoon per quart)
> 1 cup white wine

Cut fish into 1-inch pieces and cover completely with brine made of pickling salt and water. Place in refrigerator for 24 hours. Drain and rinse very well. Cover fish with vinegar for 24 hours in refrigerator. Drain but do not rinse. Save vinegar.

Boil vinegar, sugar and pickling spices (1 teaspoon per quart). After mixture comes to a boil, remove from heat, cool and add wine. Pour this mixture over fish pieces, divide into 3 1-quart jars. Onion slices can be added if you like. Store for 1 week in refrigerator before use.

Yield: 3 quarts

Cook's Note: You can make this recipe in smaller quantities.

Shrimp on Sugar Cane

Mai Nguyen ◆ Ramsey County

Shrimp:
    1 pound raw shrimp, shelled and deveined
    1 teaspoon salt
    ¼ pound ground pork
    2 cloves garlic, peeled and crushed
    3 shallots, peeled and finely chopped
    1 teaspoon sugar
    1 egg white, lightly beaten
    ½ teaspoon black pepper
    1 teaspoon cornstarch
    2 teaspoons vegetable oil
    8 sugar canes, approx. 6-inch long,
        split lengthwise into 4 pieces or skewers

Accompaniments:
    5 ounces rice vermicelli, cooked
    1 medium cucumber, diced
    1 ounce fresh cilantro, rinsed
    1 ounce fresh mint leaves, rinsed
    1 head butter lettuce, rinsed and separated into leaves
    12 sheets rice paper, softened with water
    dipping sauce

Shrimp: In a large mixing bowl add the shrimp and sprinkle with salt. Set aside for five minutes. Rinse the shrimp under cold water and dry with paper towels. Add shrimp, ground pork, salt, garlic, shallots, sugar, egg white, pepper, cornstarch and oil into the food processor. Process the mixture until it becomes a sticky paste.

Use 2 slightly heaping tablespoons shrimp paste to wrap around each sugar cane piece near the center leaving about 1-inch of the ends exposed to serve as handles. (It will look like a bundle of shrimp paste with a skewer running through the middle.)

Grill the sugar cane pieces on medium hot barbecue fire until golden brown (about 5 minutes, turning often).

Accompaniments: Mix vermicelli, cucumber, cilantro and mint leaves in a serving bowl.

Place lettuce leaf on rice paper. Remove grill shrimp paste from sugar cane skewer and place on lettuce. Add some of the vermicelli mixture, if desired, and roll up. Serve immediately with dipping sauce.

Yield: 4 to 6 servings

Dijon-Grilled Chicken Breasts

Anne Lauer ◆ Washington County

Grilling is a standard event during the Minnesota summer! I still prefer to start charcoal and use a Weber kettle grill, but gas grills work fine, too.

⅓ cup green onions, chopped
¼ cup Dijon mustard
¼ cup mayonnaise
¼ cup lemon juice
2 cloves garlic, minced
1 teaspoon dried thyme
¾ teaspoon salt
½ teaspoon pepper
8 chicken breasts, skinless and boneless

Combine onions, mustard, mayonnaise, lemon juice, garlic, dried thyme, salt and pepper in large zippered plastic bag. Add 8 chicken breasts. Refrigerate 2 hours, turning once. Grill over medium heat, 6 to 8 minutes per side.

Yield: 8 servings

Cook's Note: Serve with sliced fresh tomatoes and any garden salad ingredients that are in season.

Russian Kulebiaka

Sem Karpman ◆ Hennepin County

M any secrets of Russian cuisine were preserved in monasteries. Ortho-
dox monks created recipes that later became dishes of pride in cook-
books. "Kulebiaka," a long meat pie with a variety of fillings, is a traditional
meal served at Russian dinner tables since the 14th and 15th centuries.

In the 18th century, Russian cuisine was enriched by the addition of
French culinary influences. Famous French chefs were invited to the Im-
perial court and homes of aristocrats and were employed in restaurants.
They started making traditional Russian meals with a Western-European
flair. Kulebiaka was changed, too, and was made with puff pastry, mul-
tiple fillings and sauces.

Today, you can find many different kinds of Kulebiaka on menus at
Russian restaurants here and in Russia. It can be served as a simple
supper or for an upscale dinner party.

I grew up in Russia and studied cooking and food service in Russia
and Europe. I now live here with my family, work as a chef in the Twin
Cities and teach adult classes in fine cuisine.

2 puff pastry sheets
2 large crepes
2 egg yolks for brushing

Filling 1:

2 large onions, diced
2 teaspoons butter, clarified
2 pounds chicken thigh
meat, diced
fresh ground black pepper

kosher salt
1 clove fresh garlic, minced
1 teaspoon flour
1 teaspoon parsley, chopped

Filling 2:

5 to 6 dried porcini mushrooms
1 large onion, minced

1 pound cooked rice
3 hard boiled eggs, chopped

Filling 1: Sauté onions with butter until light brown, add the diced
chicken meat, seasonings and garlic. When the meat is cooked, add the
flour. Chill, and add the chopped parsley.

Filling 2: Soak porcini mushrooms in cold water for 2 to 3 hours. Sauté the minced onion and chopped mushrooms, mix with cooked rice and chopped hard boiled eggs, and chill.

Roll out puff pastry the long way, add filling 1, then cover with crepes. Spread filling 2 over crepes and cover with puff pastry. Crimp the edges to seal the kulebiaka.

Brush with egg yolks, and poke small holes into the crust. Decorate with little balls of puff pastry. Bake in a preheated oven until golden brown at 350° to 375° for about 30 to 35 minutes.

Yield: 10 servings

Chicken in Thai Green Curry

Wassana Mach ◆ Ramsey County

I remember my husband likes to eat Thai food. He likes to eat Chicken in Thai Green Curry. When I make, he have to say, "Thanks, my love."

1 (10-ounce) chicken breast
½ pound Thai eggplant
1 can coconut milk
2 tablespoons green curry paste
1 cup water
3 tablespoons fish sauce
1 teaspoon sugar
20 fresh basil leaves
1 medium red pepper, cut in ½-inch strips
2½ cups rice, steamed

Cut chicken into strips about ¼-inch thick, 2-inches long and 1-inch wide. Wash eggplant and cut into 8 pieces. Heat coconut milk in sauce pan until it boils. Stir in green curry paste. Add chicken, stir for 2 minutes. Add eggplant, stir. Add water, stir. Cover and simmer 20 minutes. Add fish sauce and sugar. Stir for 2 minutes. Add ¾ of basil and red pepper and stir for 1 minute. Remove from heat. Put in deep serving dish. Add remaining basil and red pepper as garnish. Serve over steamed rice.

Yield: 2 servings

Sharp Cheddar Fondue

MaryJo Boyle ◆ Washington County

Fondue is not only delicious to eat, but it's a great way to entertain, especially during a Minnesota winter. It can be prepared in advance, served as an appetizer or by itself as an entrée. People love getting together for a fondue party.

¼ cup butter
¼ cup flour
½ teaspoon salt
¼ teaspoon dry mustard
1 (12-ounce) can of beer
1½ teaspoons Worcestershire sauce
2 cups sharp Cheddar cheese, shredded
pumpernickel or sourdough bread, in bite-size pieces, optional
roasted vegetables, such as carrots, potatoes, asparagus
    or mushrooms

Melt butter in a heavy 2-quart saucepan, blend in flour, salt and dry mustard. Gradually whisk in beer and Worcestershire sauce. Cook over medium heat, stirring constantly with a wooden spoon, until mixture thickens and comes to a boil. Add cheese and continue stirring until the cheese is completely melted.

Pour into fondue pot and serve.

Yield: 2 to 4 servings

Cook's Notes: This can be made up to 2 days in advance and reheated. I serve this fondue with high-quality pumpernickel or sourdough bread, roasted vegetables such as carrots, potatoes, asparagus or mushrooms and beer, wine or apple cider.

Veggie Burgers

The Commonplace Restaurant ◆ Ramsey County

The late '60s and early '70s saw a cultural change, part of which was an interest in changing eating habits. A number of food cooperatives opened in the Twin Cities. There also were new restaurants such as The Commonplace, which operated on Selby Avenue just east of Western. They explained their philosophy as, "People with many different feelings and ideas came together to create the restaurant, but they agreed that they wanted a place where work was pleasant, where people came together cooperatively, and where nutritious, good food was available at low prices."

The Commonplace was operated as a cooperative with people sharing work and responsibilities, buying food from places like the People's Warehouse and the nearby Selby food co-op. One of its initial workers was Brenda Langdon, a St. Paul native who founded and still runs Café Brenda, one of the most well-known whole-food restaurants in the Twin Cities.

3 cups peanuts	2 cups rice, cooked
2 cups sunflower seeds	¾ cup nut yeast
2 cups sesame seeds	4 teaspoons lecithin
3 stalks celery	2 tablespoons salt
2 medium onions	¾ cup soy flour
1⅔ cups soybeans, cooked	2 tablespoons dill seeds
3 carrots	cheese slices, optional
8 cloves garlic	

Roast the peanuts, sunflower seeds and sesame seeds lightly. Grind peanuts, sunflower seeds, sesame seeds, celery, onions, soybeans, carrots and garlic together. Add remaining ingredients. Make into patties. Heat patties in an oiled skillet. You may melt cheese on top if you wish.

Yield: 50 servings

Grilled Bison Tenderloin
with Lingonberries

Brent Wennberg ◆ Ramsey County

Bison is an exquisitely delicious, healthy, natural, grass-fed lean meat. The meat is served with lingonberry glaze and lingonberry sauce in a salute to our Swedish ancestors.

Lingonberry Glaze:
  1 tablespoon extra virgin olive oil
  1 cup shallots, minced
  2 cloves garlic, minced
  2 cups red wine
  1 cup chicken broth
  2 cups lingonberry preserves
  1 tablespoon orange zest
  ¼ cup fresh sage, chopped
  1 tablespoon honey

  1 whole (4- to 5-pounds) bison tenderloin
  salt and pepper

Lingonberry Glaze: In a saucepan heat the olive oil over medium heat. Add the shallots and garlic and cook for about 7 minutes. Add the wine, increase the heat to high and boil until reduced to half. Add the chicken broth, lingonberry preserves, the orange zest and the sage until the glaze has a sauce-like consistency. Add the honey.

Prepare the tenderloin by trimming all fat and silver skin. Fold the tail of the tenderloin back onto the tenderloin and tie with kitchen string to give the meat a cylindrical shape.

Transfer the tenderloin to a baking sheet, brush generously with the glaze. Sprinkle with salt and pepper. Cover and let sit in a refrigerator for 1 to 2 hours.

Prepare grill for direct grilling and preheat to medium-high. Oil the grate on the grill. Place the tenderloin on the hot grate. Brush the tenderloin with the glaze. Grill the tenderloin until crusty and seared on all sides, 6 to 7 minutes per side, about 28 minutes in all. The tenderloin is done when an instant-read thermometer, inserted into the thickest part of the tenderloin reads 145° (for medium rare). Brush the tenderloin generously with the glaze during the last 5 minutes of grilling.

Transfer the tenderloin to a cutting board, cover loosely with aluminum foil, and let rest 5 minutes. Remove the string and carve the tenderloin into crosswise slices and serve with the remaining lingonberry glaze and lingonberry spread.

Yield: 6 to 8 servings

Cook's Note: We serve this dish at Thanksgiving or Christmas together with turkey, crème fraische-mashed potatoes, pan gravy, traditional side dishes and a fine Pinot Noir.

Very Hot Chicken

Tela A. Gebremedhin ◆ Ramsey County

We make this chicken for big parties. My mother made it for my family during Easter and for Christmas. In Ethiopia, we serve it with a special drink made with honey.

2 onions, chopped
3 potatoes, washed and peeled
3 carrots, washed, peeled and chopped
2 habañero peppers, chopped
½ cup garlic
¼ cup vegetable oil
1 tablespoon butter
1 gallon water
1 whole chicken, washed and dried

Preheat oven to 350°. Mix all ingredients, except the chicken, together in an oven-proof bowl. Pour mixture over the fresh chicken, making sure to cover all parts of the poultry. Cover the bowl and place in oven. Bake for 3 hours, basting with the liquid every ½ hour or so, until chicken is tender and golden brown.

Yield: 4 to 6 servings

Pheasant in a Crock

Chris Schlueter ◆ McLeod County

Minnesota has a lot of good pheasant hunting areas. My husband is an avid hunter, so we eat a lot of pheasant. This is great for a Sunday dinner or for company.

> 1 (2- to 3-pound) pheasant, rinsed and patted dry
> 3 to 4 sprigs fresh thyme
> 3 sprigs fresh parsley
> 2 garlic cloves — 1 crushed and 1 sliced
> salt
> fresh ground pepper
> zest of 1 large orange in long curly strips
> 1 large orange, halved and squeezed, juice reserved
> 4 slices smoky bacon
> 1 tablespoon olive oil
> ¼ cup chicken broth

Put the thyme, parsley, crushed garlic and 1 orange half inside the pheasant. Tuck the garlic slices between the legs and body. Season the pheasant with the salt and pepper. Lay orange zest over the breast. Wrap the breast with bacon and put the pheasant in a slow cooker. Pour reserved orange juice over the bird. Drizzle the pheasant with olive oil and broth. Cover and cook on high for 3 ½ to 5 hours or until the meat is tender and an instant-read meat thermometer inserted in the thigh registers 180°.

Serve on a platter with the juices poured over.

Yield: 1 pheasant

Calico Beans

Joretta Machmeier ◆ Chisago County

I have been cooking for my husband and family for more than 55 years. I asked my husband about his favorite recipe and his answer was, "Calico Beans!" It's also popular at family get-togethers, church suppers and potlucks. Make it part of a picnic beside one of Minnesota's 10,000 lakes.

1 cup onions, chopped
1 pound ground beef
½ pound bacon, chopped
½ cup ketchup
¼ cup brown sugar, packed
dash chili powder
1 teaspoon salt
1 teaspoon mustard
2 teaspoons vinegar
1 (1-pound) can of pork and beans
1 (15-ounce) can of kidney beans
1 (8-ounce) can of lima beans, drained

Brown onion, ground beef and bacon. Add the remaining ingredients. Bake at 350° for 1 hour.

Yield: 8 to 10 servings

Cook's Note: For a picnic menu, serve grilled hamburger on a bun, calico beans, potato salad, apple pie, lemonade and coffee.

Chicken Chili

Mikki Krueger—First Baptist Church ◆ Isanti County

This chili is fun to serve after you've cut down a fresh Christmas tree. There's just enough "heat" to warm you after being chilled by Minnesota's winter air! Make it ahead and share with family and friends.

3 whole chicken breasts, boned and skinned
1 cup onion, chopped
1 green pepper, chopped
3 cloves garlic, minced
¾ teaspoon cumin (adds heat)
¾ teaspoon chili powder
½ teaspoon salt
1 teaspoon basil
2 (15-ounce) cans Mexican-style canned tomatoes
    and green chilies
1 (15-ounce) can black beans, drained
1 (8-ounce) can pinto beans
small can corn
3 tablespoons lime juice (adds heat)
cheese, grated
sour cream

Heat a large pan sprayed with non-stick spray over medium-high heat. Add chicken, onion, green pepper and garlic. Sauté 5 to 7 minutes until chicken is no longer pink. Add seasonings, tomatoes, black beans, pinto beans, corn and lime juice and simmer for 20 minutes. Serve with grated cheese and sour cream.

Yield: 6 to 8 servings

Hamburger, Wild Rice and Sauerkraut Hotdish

Maryann Porter ◆ Carver County

In 2007, Waconia celebrated its 150-year anniversary with a Minnesota Cook Off. I entered this recipe in the hotdish category and won first place. Lt. Gov. Molnau and Eric Perkins from KARE-11 TV were two of the celebrity judges for the event. Inspiration for this recipe came from my grandmother, who took the time when I was a child to share with me her wonderful cooking and baking skills. It incorporates wild rice — Minnesota's state grain — and sauerkraut, which celebrates the German heritage of the Waconia area.

> 2 pounds ground beef
> 1 medium onion, diced
> 1 (14-ounce) can sauerkraut, drained
> 2 (6-ounce) packages Long Grain Wild Rice (ready rice in a pouch)
> 1 (2½-ounce) container of Asiago cheese, shredded
> 2 (10¾-ounce) cans cream of celery soup
> 1 (6-ounce) can fried onions

Brown ground beef and onion. Remove from stove and drain off excess fat. Mix in sauerkraut, rice, cheese and soup. Put in a 9x13-inch casserole dish. Bake uncovered at 350º for 45 minutes. Sprinkle fried onions on top and bake for another 15 minutes.

Yield: 6 servings

Itasca Jambalaya

Pam G. Harris ◆ Hennepin County

I like the way this recipe unites two ends of the Mississippi River with ingredients from Minnesota and Louisiana.

1 cup Minnesota wild rice
3 cups chicken or vegetable broth
salt and pepper, to taste
1 tablespoon shortening
1 pound hot turkey sausage, cut into ½-inch slices
1 large onion, chopped
1 tablespoon flour
3 cups canned tomatoes, diced
2½ cups water
½ cup red bell pepper, chopped
1 garlic clove, minced
1¼ teaspoons salt
½ teaspoon thyme
¼ teaspoon red pepper
2 tablespoons Worcestershire sauce
3 cups shrimp, cooked
2 tablespoons parsley, chopped

Rinse rice well. Place in casserole, add broth, stir and bake at 375° covered for 35 to 45 minutes. Uncover and continue baking until all liquid is absorbed, about 15 minutes. Season with salt and pepper. May be done ahead and refrigerated until needed.

Melt shortening in large skillet or Dutch oven. Add sausage and onion, cook, stirring often for 5 minutes. Stir in flour until smooth. Cook for 1 to 2 minutes longer. Add tomatoes, water, bell pepper, garlic and parsley. Cook to the boiling point. Stir in baked rice and seasonings and simmer until heated, 20 minutes or so. Add cooked, thawed shrimp and heat through being careful not to over cook. Sprinkle each serving with chopped parsley.

Yield: 6 to 8 servings

Cook's Note: I revised an old recipe to make it acceptable to a non-meat eating daughter. We serve this dish at Christmas with a salad and a good local beer like Summit.

Wild Rice Chicken Hotdish

Elaine Hugill ◆ Hennepin County

1 large onion, chopped
1 cup celery, diced
1 clove garlic, minced (optional)
½ cup butter
2 cups chicken broth
2 cups chicken, cooked and cubed
1 large can sliced mushrooms (optional)
6 cups cooked wild rice (for more flavor you can cook
   the wild rice in chicken broth)
½ cup almonds, slivered
salt and pepper to taste

Sauté the onions, celery and garlic in butter until tender. Add the chicken broth, chicken, mushrooms, rice and almonds. Salt and pepper to taste. Bake in an ungreased casserole dish at 350° for 30 to 45 minutes, or put in large slow cooker and cook on low for 3 to 4 hours.

Yield: Fills a large slow cooker, so it serves 12 to 15

Cook's Note: We usually make this after Thanksgiving and substitute chopped turkey for the chicken. We like to cook the wild rice until it "pearls out." The rice grains open up and are more tender.

Pork Chop Stew

Maria King ◆ Anoka County

This stew makes a great camping meal. It smells wonderful, especially when I cook it over a campfire while my family is out on the lake fishing. One time, the wind carried the aroma across the water, and several strangers, who had been out on the lake, stopped by our campsite to ask what's for dinner! It turned out to be a good way to meet new friends.

> 4 pork chops
> salt, pepper and garlic to taste
> 1 medium onion, diced
> 4 potatoes, peeled and cubed
> 1 pound of carrots, diced
> 1 envelope onion soup mix
> 1 package powdered beef gravy mix
> water to cover the meat and vegetables
> additional vegetables according to your family's liking—
>   peas, broccoli, cauliflower, corn, cabbage, etc.
> 1 (8-ounce) carton sour cream or a package
>   powdered sour cream mix

Brown the chops and season with salt, pepper and garlic. Add onions, potatoes and carrots. Carrots may be fresh or out of a can. Add dry onion soup mix, powdered beef gravy mix and enough water to cover the veggies in the pan. Boil gently until the vegetables are done. If done while camping, simmer at the back of the campfire for 20 to 30 minutes. Add sour cream just before serving and don't let it boil again or the cream will separate.

Yield: 4 servings

Cook's Note: This is a meal in itself, but you can round it out with bread and dessert.

Doris Rubenstein's Infamous State-Fair Reject Authentic Kosher Dill Pickles

Doris Rubenstein ◆ Hennepin County

This is a folk recipe that's still made in the home and not often found in stores or even at farmers' markets. It represents the food of the Jewish people that have been a part of Minnesota since before statehood. This recipe has gone around the world thanks to National Public Radio and other media who covered the story about the recipe and how it lost during State Fair judging in 2000.

> pickling cucumbers
> 1 ½ tablespoons coarse kosher salt
> 1 clove garlic
> 1 teaspoon pickling spice
> 2 sprigs of dill
> 1 small cayenne pepper
> water

Place all ingredients but one sprig of dill in a sterilized quart canning jar. Pack pickles in tightly and top with the other sprig of dill. Fill the jar with clean cold water. Seal tightly and shake until salt is dissolved. Store in a cool, dark place for 2 weeks. The salt and ambient yeast will preserve and ferment the cucumbers. Do not be concerned if the lid fizzes or if sediment appears at the bottom to make the brine cloudy. This is part of the fermentation process.

Yield: One jar yields 10 servings

Cook's Note: These pickles pair perfectly with delicatessen foods such as corned beef or pastrami sandwiches or hot dogs.

Coon Rapids Carrot Cake

Laura Troiber ◆ Anoka County

This recipe is a celebration of tradition. It came from my great-grand-mother, the first of five generations of our family to live in Coon Rapids. I found it and updated it to enhance the flavor and make it my own — I just couldn't use 1½ cups oil in a cake! It's become one of my signature dishes, and I look forward to sharing it with my daughter when she begins to cook. This cake makes a wonderful dessert anytime, and it's great for potlucks.

Cake:

1 can (20-ounce) crushed pineapple, drained, reserve juice
1 cup golden raisins
¾ cup oil (not olive)
¾ cup applesauce, unsweetened
1½ cups sugar
3 eggs
1 pound carrots, grated
1 teaspoon vanilla
2½ cups flour
1 teaspoon soda
½ teaspoon salt
1 teaspoon cinnamon
¼ teaspoon nutmeg or cloves or ground ginger (this is the "what ever I have" ingredient) optional
1 cup nuts, chopped (walnuts or pecans)

Frosting:

6 ounces cream cheese, softened (light works great)
2 cups powdered sugar
¼ cup butter
¼ teaspoon vanilla

Cake: Preheat oven to 350°. Drain pineapple and reserve juice. Soak raisins in the juice, set aside. Combine oil, applesauce, sugar and eggs. Mix well. Stir in carrots, drained pineapple and vanilla. Add flour, soda, salt, cinnamon and "optional spice." Stir until well blended. Drain raisins. Mix raisins and nuts into batter. Spread in greased and floured 9x13-inch pan. Bake until toothpick comes out clean, about 30 to 40 minutes. Let cool and frost.

Frosting: Combine frosting ingredients and blend until smooth. Spread on cooled cake. Yum!

Yield: 24 servings

Cook's Note: This also makes great cupcakes. Some ingredients, like nuts, are optional, or you can add others, like chopped dates or apricots. Have some fun with it!

Grandma Godfrey's Gingerbread

Ard Godfrey House ◆ Hennepin County

Ard Godfrey helped build the first dam and sawmill using St. Anthony Falls. His wife, Harriet, is credited with bringing dandelions to Minnesota by importing seeds from Maine. She used dandelions to make bread and tea. Their home, the Ard Godfrey House, is the oldest wood frame house remaining in Minneapolis; it was moved to its present location – Chute Square – in 1909.

½ cup shortening	2½ cups flour
1 cup molasses	1 teaspoon soda
1 cup sour cream	1 teaspoon salt
1 egg, beaten	1 teaspoon ginger

Beat shortening while adding molasses gradually. Stir in sour cream. Add egg. Sift together dry ingredients and stir in. Pour into greased and floured 9-inch pan. Bake in a preheated oven at 325° for 50 minutes or until wooden pick inserted in the center comes out clean.

Yield: 9 servings

Chocolate Malted Milk Cookies

Maureen Athman ♦ Benton County

Graduation parties are a big neighborhood event here. Each party has a spread of different cookies brought by families. Betty Janson makes this recipe, three batches at a time. She freezes the cookies for graduation parties, church gatherings and offers them to anyone who stops by to visit.

1 cup shortening or butter
1 ¼ cups brown sugar
1 egg
½ cup malted milk powder (not chocolate)
2 tablespoons chocolate syrup
1 tablespoon vanilla
1 teaspoon baking soda
½ teaspoon salt
2 ¼ cups flour
2 cups chocolate chips (or chocolate chunks)

Cream together butter and brown sugar. Add egg and cream together. Stir in malted milk powder, chocolate syrup and vanilla; mix well. Combine baking soda, salt and flour and add to creamed mixture; mix well. Drop by teaspoonful on to ungreased cookie sheets. Bake at 300° for 10 to 12 minutes. Make a test cookie to check for adequate flour.

Yield: 3 dozen cookies

Cranberry Oatmeal Cookies

Deborah Kreger ♦ Sherburne County

The men and women in my National Guard unit made this the most-requested cookie for annual training. As one of the guys said "I can take a handful of these cookies, and they make a great breakfast." I still make them in a triple batch.

⅔ cup butter-flavored shortening
4 teaspoons water
⅔ cup brown sugar, packed
2 eggs
1½ cups oats
1½ cups flour
1 teaspoon baking soda
½ teaspoon salt
½ teaspoon cinnamon to taste
¼ teaspoon nutmeg to taste
1½ cups dried cranberries
⅔ cup white or chocolate chips

Cream together shortening, water and sugar until fluffy. Add eggs. Sift dry ingredients and mix in. Stir in cranberries and chips. Drop by rounded teaspoonfuls onto ungreased cookie sheets. Bake in a preheated oven about 10 minutes at 375°.

Yield: 3 to 4 dozen cookies

Cook's Note: Use raisins and cinnamon chips instead of dried cranberries and white chips. My sons prefer I skip the fruit and use chocolate chips. These cookies also freeze well.

Grandma Who Who's Strawberry Cookies

Julie Weidenborner ◆ Sherburne County

This recipe is from my Grandmother Eleanor (Eischens) Savard – better known as Grandma Who Who to my children because she always answered a knock at her door by saying, "Who who?" When she was a young girl growing up on a farm in western Minnesota, her father was stricken with tuberculosis. This was a devastating disease that killed thousands and wreaked havoc on many families. Not only did the disease take the life of my great-grandfather, the family lost their farm, and the children scattered looking for work.

My grandmother moved to St. Paul to attend beauty school. To put herself through school, she cooked and cleaned for several families in the area. These families presented her with beautiful plates of cookies during the Christmas season as a thank you gift for her hard work. Many were traditional family recipes. That tradition of the Christmas Cookie Platter eventually became the Christmas Cookie Tin and is still being passed on in our family.

The Christmas Tins are now in their fourth generation and are given as gifts to our close family and friends. The tins contain many of the original cookie recipes that my grandmother collected as a young girl and ones of her own that she added. They are both beautiful and delicious. These Christmas cookies serve as a reminder of our past, how precious life is and how meaningful gifts are that come from the heart.

We still fight over these strawberry cookies at our family Christmas parties. When we were kids, Grandma only put out four at a time, and all of us would make a mad scramble for them. I think she loved this part most about Christmas at her house. Miraculously everyone got a strawberry by the end of the night, but that was always our little secret.

Cookies:
1 pound coconut
1 pound almonds without skins
1 can sweetened condensed milk
2 tablespoons sugar
1 (6-ounce) package of dry strawberry gelatin (divided)
1 to 2 tablespoons almond extract
red food coloring

Frosting, optional:
margarine
powdered sugar
green food coloring

Cookies: Finely grind the coconut and almonds and mix them together using a food processor or hand grinder. Just make sure they are ground very fine so that they will hold their shape and form. Add the can of sweetened condensed milk, sugar, ¾ of the large gelatin mix, almond flavoring and red food coloring as desired to the coconut and almond mixture. Mix well; cover tightly and refrigerate over night.

The next day shape the dough into strawberries by rolling 1-inch balls of dough in your palms leaving the top wider than the bottom. Roll the strawberry shape into the remaining bowl of dry strawberry gelatin and let dry on wax paper.

Frosting: You may add frosting leaves by mixing margarine and powdered sugar together until it forms a paste. Add green food coloring to make the desired color. Take a butter knife and dab the top of the strawberries with some of the green frosting to form leaves. Let the strawberries with frosting leaves set on wax paper and store them in a safe place until Christmas.

Yield: 2 to 3 dozen

Peanut Cups

Donna V. Lardy ◆ Stearns County

These are a favorite at Christmas.

1 (16-ounce) package chocolate almond bark
1 cup chunky peanut butter
1 (12-ounce) package real chocolate chips

Heat and stir almond bark in a double boiler until melted. Stir in peanut butter and chocolate chips. Heat and stir until all are melted. Drop by teaspoonfuls into miniature paper baking cups and cool until hard.

Yield: 20 to 40 servings

PBM Chocolate Chip Cookies

Beverly Barrett ◆ Meeker County

L itchfield has been part of a Peanut Butter & Milk exchange since 1971. Every fall a delegation from Meeker County goes to Hartford, AL, to experience southern culture. Hartford guests visit Litchfield in February to experience northern hospitality, participate in winter activities and tour farms and local business. During the week, lots of dairy products and peanut butter recipes are served. It doesn't get much better than great-tasting chocolate chip cookies with peanut butter, like this recipe from my daughter.

½ cup butter
½ cup sugar
⅓ cup brown sugar, packed
½ cup peanut butter
½ teaspoon vanilla extract
1 egg
1 cup flour
1 teaspoon baking soda
¼ teaspoon salt
½ cup rolled oats
1 cup semisweet chocolate chips

Preheat oven to 350° degrees.

In a medium bowl, cream together the butter, sugar and brown sugar until smooth. Stir in peanut butter, vanilla and egg until well blended. Combine the flour, baking soda, and salt; stir into the batter just until moistened. Mix in the oats and chocolate chips until evenly distributed. Drop by tablespoonfuls onto lightly greased cookie sheets.

Bake for 10 to 12 minutes, until the edges start to brown. Cool on cookie sheets for about 5 minutes before transferring to wire racks to cool completely.

Yield: 24 to 30 cookies

Swedish Kringla

Amy Wilde—County Commissioner ◆ Meeker County

This is an old Swedish recipe, but it's still regularly served at Christmas, St. Lucia's Day, Scandinavian Midsummer's Day events and Scandinavian buffets. It's adapted slightly from a recipe by Mrs. Arvid Bergquist of Dassel.

Kringla:
   2 cups flour
   1 cup butter
   2 tablespoons + 1 cup water
   3 eggs
   ½ teaspoon almond extract

Frosting:
   1 cup powdered sugar
   1 tablespoon butter, softened
   ½ teaspoon almond extract
   2 to 3 tablespoons milk or cream
   1 to 1 ½ cups almonds, chopped or slivered

Kringla: Blend 1 cup flour, ½ cup butter and 2 tablespoons of water until thoroughly mixed and pat out onto a cookie sheet in 2 long strips, about 3-inches wide. Heat 1 cup water and the other ½ cup butter to boiling. Remove from heat and immediately add the other cup of flour and stir until smooth. Add eggs, 1 at a time, and beat well after each addition. Add ½ teaspoon of almond extract. Spread this mixture on the dough strips. Bake in a preheated oven at 350° for 55 to 60 minutes. Cool and frost.

Frosting: Mix powdered sugar, softened butter and almond extract. Add enough milk or cream to spread. Sprinkle chopped or slivered almonds on top. (Cake decors may be substituted for the nuts.)

Yield: 3 dozen pieces

Braham Pie Day Crust

Marilyn McGriff ◆ Isanti County

This is the pie crust recipe used for the annual Braham Pie Day, which began as a Celebrate Minnesota event in 1990.

20 cups (5 pounds) flour
2 teaspoons salt
3 pound can vegetable shortening or 3 pounds lard
2½ cups water
½ cup vinegar

Combine flour and salt in a big bowl. Cut in shortening or lard with pastry blender until well blended. Combine vinegar and water and add all at once to flour/shortening mixture. Mix well. Divide dough into 20 oblong rolls (each about 8 ounces). Wrap in plastic wrap and freeze what you don't immediately need. Use within 12 months.

Yield: 20 single-crust pies or 10 double-crust pies (at 7 slices per pie, this could be enough for 140 happy eaters!)

Cook's Note: Little measuring is necessary with the 5-pound bag of flour and the 3-pound can of shortening; the vinegar assures easy rolling. With the logs of crust in the freezer, making a dessert is as easy as "pie."

SOUTHEAST REGION

When you're in the Southeast, you're in farm country.
Dairy farms, corn-soybean-and-wheat farms, big family farms and small specialty farms. Farms where robust meals satisfy hearty appetites whetted by day-long physical labor. With the farms come fairs and festivals where 4-Hers enter their food projects and cooks proudly submit their baked goods, preserves and pickles, all hoping to bring home the coveted blue ribbon. You'll find this home cooking on display at community and church suppers and quaint B&Bs tucked into small towns throughout the region, too.

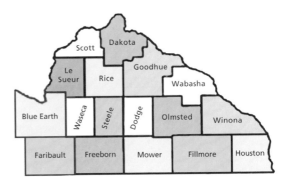

Green Chili Dip

Kathy Hoeft ◆ Olmsted County

G reat for parties!

1 (4-ounce) can green chilies, chopped
1 (4-ounce) can black olives, chopped
2 (8-ounce) packages of cream cheese, softened
½ cup sour cream
1 small bunch green onions, chopped fine
½ cup of your favorite salsa
chopped or minced garlic to taste (start with 1 teaspoon)
tortilla chips

Mix all ingredients together. Let chill overnight for best flavor.

Yield: 1 quart

Cook's Note: Lowfat cream cheese and sour cream can be used with this recipe. Serve with tortilla or corn chips.

Honey Dip for Veggies

Jeanette E. Anderson ◆ Rice County

1 ½ cups mayonnaise
7 drops hot pepper sauce
2 tablespoons honey
2 tablespoons ketchup
2 tablespoons onion, minced
2 tablespoons lemon juice
1 teaspoon curry powder
assorted veggies cut into bite-sized pieces

Combine all ingredients except veggies. Blend thoroughly, refrigerate and serve with fresh veggies.

Yield: 6 to 8 servings

Spinach Walnut Feta Quiche

Lisa Durkee ◆ Blue Earth County

The Amboy Cottage Café is a 1928 gas station that we renovated, and the town of Amboy has adopted it as a gathering place. It's well known for its old-fashioned home cooking and community support. Tuesday is "Quiche Day" at The Cottage, and I've developed several that have become favorites. This is our seventh year in business, and we plan to continue for many more.

1 unbaked 9-inch pie crust
1 medium onion, chopped
2 tablespoons olive oil
3 garlic cloves, chopped
1 cup feta cheese, crumbled
3 eggs
1 ½ cups half-and-half
½ teaspoon salt
¾ cup walnuts, chopped
1 pound frozen spinach, thawed and chopped

In a skillet, sauté onions in olive oil until translucent; add garlic and sauté 30 seconds. Toss into a bowl, add remaining ingredients and combine thoroughly. Pour into pie crust and bake in a preheated oven at 350° for 30 to 45 minutes, or until set and browned. Serve warm.

Yield: 6 servings

Cook's Note: I usually start the meal with a fresh tossed salad, then serve a generous slice of Spinach Walnut Feta Quiche, homemade oat-and-wheat bread and a side of butter-baked potato or garlic pasta.

Coconut Bread

Teresa Smith - The Historic Anderson House ◆ Wabasha County

Bread:
   4 eggs
   2 cups sugar
   1 cup vegetable oil
   1 teaspoon coconut extract
   3 cups flour
   ½ teaspoon baking powder
   ½ teaspoon baking soda
   1 cup buttermilk
   1 cup coconut
   1 cup nuts, if desired

Glaze:
   1½ cups sugar
   3 tablespoons butter
   ¾ cup water
   1 teaspoon coconut extract

Preheat oven to 325°. Spray 2 9x5-inch loaf pans with nonstick cooking spray, lightly flour.

Bread: In large bowl, combine eggs, sugar, oil and extract. Gradually stir in flour, baking powder and baking soda alternately with buttermilk. Stir in coconut and nuts. Pour mixture in prepared pans. Bake 1 hour or until toothpick inserted in center comes out clean. Cool slightly in pans on wire rack, remove from pans.

Glaze: Combine all ingredients in medium saucepan. Heat to boiling; cook 5 minutes, stirring occasionally. Pour over warm breads. Let stand 3 to 4 hours. Store in refrigerator.

Yield: 2 loaves

Houska
(Czechoslovakian Christmas Bread)

Marilyn Carrigan ◆ Freeborn County

This houska recipe is from my grandmother, Josephine Belskan, of rural Myrtle. Myrtle is a Czechoslovakian (Bohemian) community. For years Kolacky Days were celebrated at the local ZCBJ Hall. This is traditional bread baked at Christmas. Originally it was made with duck grease instead of shortening.

2 packages quick rise dry yeast mix
¼ cup warm water
2 cups milk, scalded
1 cup sugar
7 cups flour
1 cup shortening
5 teaspoons lemon extract
1 ½ cups raisins
1 container of citron
2 teaspoons salt
2 eggs
1 egg yolk
4 tablespoons water
poppy seeds

Mix dry yeast with water, let stand. Heat milk until a skin forms on top. Add sugar to milk and cool. Add 2 cups flour and yeast mixture to milk; beat well and add the shortening, lemon extract, raisins, citron, salt, eggs and remaining 5 cups of flour. Knead into a soft dough (with lightly oiled hands.) Let dough rise until doubled. Punch down and let rise again. Shape bread into 2 or 3 loaves. Let rise before baking. Brush top with mixture of 1 egg yolk and 4 tablespoons of water. Sprinkle generously with poppy seeds. Bake in a preheated oven at 350° approximately 35 to 40 minutes until dark golden brown on top.

Yield: 2 or 3 loaves

Cook's Notes: Serve with or without butter.

Blue Ribbon Cream Cheese Coffee Cake

Barb Schaller ◆ Dakota County

In the late 1980s and early 1990s, I received four blue ribbons for my coffee cake at the Minnesota State Fair. The last time it won, I had intended to enter something else. But when the other recipe turned out to be a colossal failure, at the last moment I pulled one of these coffee-cakes from my freezer and entered it instead. It had been in the freezer for about six weeks, and when my son and I saw the blue ribbon, we laughed uproariously. I hadn't expected it to win anything. That's when I decided to tell everyone that "it freezes beautifully."

Crust:
> 1 packet active dry yeast
> ¼ cup water, very warm
> ¼ cup scalded milk
> 2 tablespoons sugar
> ½ teaspoon salt
> ¼ cup butter, softened
> 1 egg
> 1¾ (up to 2½) cups flour

Filling:
> 1 (8-ounce) package cream cheese, softened
> ½ cup sugar
> 1 egg
> 1 teaspoon vanilla extract

Topping:
> ¾ cup sugar
> 1 cup flour
> ½ cup butter

Powdered Sugar Icing:
> 1½ cups powdered sugar, sifted
> 3 tablespoons water
> ½ teaspoon vanilla

Crust: Dissolve yeast in warm water, let cool. Combine the milk, sugar, salt, and butter. Add yeast to milk mixture. Add the egg and flour to the yeast mixture (dough will be soft and sticky.) Place in a greased bowl and let rise until double, about 30 to 45 minutes.

Filling: While dough is rising make filling by creaming the cheese and sugar together and adding the egg and vanilla.

Topping: Combine sugar and flour and cut in butter with pastry blender until crumbly.

Powdered Sugar Icing: Combine powdered sugar, water and vanilla.

Divide dough in half and pat or roll each half into a circle and place in an 8-inch foil cake pan. Pour half the filling evenly over each pan of prepared dough. Let rise for 30 minutes. Sprinkle with topping. Bake in the middle of a preheated oven at 375° for 20 to 25 minutes, until crust begins to brown just a little. Drizzle with powdered sugar icing.

Yield: 2 (8-inch) coffee cakes, 6 to 8 servings per cake

Cook's Note: The coffee cakes freeze beautifully.

Marmalade Bread

Nancy Steele ◆ Blue Earth County

> 3 cups flour, sifted
> 1 tablespoon baking powder
> 1 teaspoon salt
> ¼ teaspoon baking soda
> 1½ cups orange marmalade
> 1 egg, beaten
> ¾ cup orange juice
> ¼ cup salad oil
> 1 cup walnuts, chopped

Sift together flour, baking powder, salt and baking soda. Reserve ¼ cup of the marmalade. Combine remaining 1¼ cups marmalade, beaten egg, orange juice and oil; add to flour mixture, stirring just until mixture is moistened. Stir in chopped nuts.

Turn batter into a greased 9x5x3-inch loaf pan. Bake in a preheated oven at 350° for about 1 hour, or until a wooden pick or cake tester inserted in center comes out clean. Transfer from loaf pan to a baking sheet. Spread reserved marmalade over top of loaf and return to oven for 1 to 2 minutes, until glazed. Cool on cake rack.

Yield: 1 loaf

Mother's Povatica (Potica)

Emily Marincel Amberg ♦ Scott County

A walnut-filled bread delicious for breakfast or coffee break.

Potica:
- ¾ cup butter, cut in pieces
- 2 cups hot water
- 2¼ teaspoons salt
- 6 tablespoons sugar
- 2 packages of dry yeast
- ½ cup warm water
- 10 to 12 cups of flour
- 3 eggs, beaten
- oil
- cinnamon, for dusting

Filling:
- ¾ cup butter
- 1½ cups milk
- 1 pound walnuts, ground fine
- 2 cups brown sugar, packed
- 2 cups sugar
- 3 large eggs, room temperature, beaten
- 1 tablespoon vanilla

Potica: In large bowl mix butter, hot water, salt and sugar. Stir until butter is melted. Let cool to warm. While cooling, dissolve dry yeast in ½ cup warm water. Add 2 cups flour to the first mixture to make a paste. Add the dissolved yeast and mix in. Add 3 beaten eggs (warmed to room temperature) and mix in. Add enough flour, about 8 to 10 cups, until dough is not sticky and is waxy looking. The flour is added gradually as dough is being kneaded; takes about 10 to 15 minutes of kneading.

Place dough in a lightly oiled bowl and turn dough to coat with oil. Cover with wax paper and cloth and let sit in a warm place until doubled in size. While waiting, make the filling.

Filling: Stir butter, milk and walnuts together in heavy saucepan. Begin to heat slowly and add the sugars. Keep cooking over low heat and add the eggs and vanilla. Cook until fairly thick and glossy, darker brown in color. Set aside and let cool a little.

To assemble: Preheat oven to 350°. Place raised dough on a large table covered with a well-floured cloth. Let rest 5 minutes. Sprinkle dough generously with flour. Roll out, going round and round until about ⅛-inch thick. Spread filling carefully on dough leaving 1- to 2-inches bare on one long side. Dust lightly with cinnamon. Start from the opposite long side, rollup toward the bare edge with a tucking under motion. Tuck in ends. Brush on milk for glue to seal edge. Cut roll in 2 pieces and place each in a greased 9x13-inch baking pan in a "U" shape. Cover with a cloth and let rise to double. Brush with milk and bake for 45 minutes. To test if done, "thump" with fingers, bread should sound hollow.

Cook's Note: Roll dough lightly with rolling pin and then gently stretch over table with hands. Should be able to see through the dough.

Clovia Pizza Dough

Susan Scruggs ◆ Blue Earth County

This recipe is from my sister-in-law's college sorority at the University of Minnesota-St. Paul. You'll never order deep-dish pizza from a restaurant again after tasting this delicious homemade creation! It's great for movie night with the family, and the kids can help make it.

Dough:	Topping:
2½ cups flour, divided	Spaghetti sauce
1 package instant dry yeast	Cheese
1½ teaspoons salt	Meat
1 cup warm water	
2 tablespoons vegetable oil	

Dough: Mix 1 cup flour, dry yeast and salt; add warm water and vegetable oil and mix until smooth. Gradually stir in additional 1½ cups of flour to make a stiff dough. Knead gently 1 to 2 minutes; let dough rest for 15 minutes. Grease a 9x13-inch pan; press dough into pan forming an outer ridge.

Topping: Add toppings as desired. Bake at 400° for 30 minutes or until light golden brown with crisp edges.

Yield: 6 servings

Cook's Note: Serve with garlic toast and a salad.

English Muffins

Shirley Anderson ◆ Olmsted County

When I graduated from Iowa State University during World War II, I was offered a job as a home economist at Pillsbury. I answered phone calls from consumers, tested recipes using Pillsbury products and developed recipes for magazines. When we were photographing foods, such as a cake, we'd make "stand-ins" until the photographer got the lighting right. The best cake would be saved for last, and its photo would appear in the magazines. When we were developing recipes, we'd make them, and then the men from advertising and others would taste our creations and decide which they liked best.

Of course, this was before bread machines. If you wanted to make bread you had to knead and keep kneading the dough with your hands. So we made a recipe book called, *Bake the No-Knead Way*, that cut bread-making down to one process. You just mixed up the ingredients and put the bread in the oven. This recipe comes from that book.

Because I sent out letters and recipes to people, I had to sign them "Ann Pillsbury," – not my name – and learned to sign just like "Ann." It was fun, but when my husband came back from the war, I resigned and went back to Iowa State and worked in the extension office.

1 cup scalded milk
¼ cup shortening
2 teaspoons salt
1 tablespoon light corn syrup
1 package yeast, dry granular or compressed
3 cups flour
4 tablespoons corn meal

In a large bowl, combine milk, shortening, salt and corn syrup. Let cool to lukewarm. Stir in yeast and mix well. Gradually add 3 cups flour, mixing until dough is well-blended and soft. On a floured surface, roll out dough to ¼-inch thickness and cut with a 3½-inch round cutter. Sprinkle a baking sheet with 2 tablespoons corn meal and place muffin rounds on the sheet. Dust muffins with remaining corn meal. Let rise in a warm place (80-85°), about 1 hour. Bake on a hot, ungreased griddle or in a large skillet, reducing heat when muffins begin to brown. Bake about 7 minutes on each side. Split the cooled muffins and serve toasted.

Yield: 10 to 12 muffins

Firehouse Potato Soup

Ramona Leonard ◆ Olmsted County

This recipe was a favorite of my husband, Don Leonard. He served more than 30 years – many of those as captain – with the Rochester fire department on the ladder truck. One of our grandchildren wrote this story:

When I asked my grandma what the guys liked to eat while they were at the hall, she said they were real "meat-and-potatoes" guys. Birthdays and holidays were big. On Thanksgiving and Christmas, those on duty would make a big holiday feast. When it was my grandpa's birthday, my grandma would bring in his favorite – yellow cake with peanut butter frosting.

One of the firefighters my grandpa worked with gave this story to my grandma: "I remember responding with Captain Don to a 'smoke on third floor.' When we arrived, people were coming out of the building with their possessions in their arms. On the third floor we saw smoke in the hallway. Captain Don pounded on every door and used his booming voice to tell everyone, 'Open your windows to clear the smoke, then get out!' One small Vietnamese man opened his door, then opened his window and threw a leg over the sill. Don pulled the guy from the windowsill and gave him a gentle shove toward the stairs."

"Oh, the source of the smoke? A lady was cooking chicken in the oven using sticks and coal."

2 (10½-ounce) cans beef broth
2 cans water
1 pound ground beef
1 teaspoon salt
dash of pepper
3 medium potatoes, peeled and sliced ¼-inch thick
1 (10-ounce) package frozen mixed vegetables
½ cup barley, optional

In large pot bring beef broth and water to boil. Season ground beef with salt and pepper. Shape into marble sized meat balls and drop meat balls into simmering broth. Add potatoes and frozen mixed vegetables to soup. Add barley if desired. Cook 10 to 15 minutes or until potatoes are tender.

Yield: Approximately 1½ quarts

Wild Rice Salad

Jana Soeldner Danger ◆ Waseca County

When my husband and I were dating, he told me about growing up in Grand Rapids and watching Native Americans harvest wild rice. He recalled they would float slowly in canoes through the rice, bending the stalks over and knocking the kernels into the bottoms of their boats with long sticks.

I grew up in Waseca, where at that time wild rice seemed quite exotic, and the story of the harvest made it seem even more so. When my husband and I married, we moved to Harris, a town of about 500 people. I discovered that I loved to spend time cooking and experimenting with ingredients.

I also discovered I could get reasonably priced Minnesota wild rice in large Minneapolis grocery stores, but in those years, it was only available in the fall. We quickly grew to love the dusky, nutty flavor of this grain that is really a grass, and we would eagerly anticipate the arrival of the new crop. When the rice came in, I would invest in enough to last for several months.

Although we ate wild rice most often as a side dish with meat, poultry or game, I began experimenting with other ways to use it. This salad is one of the results. Whenever I serve it, people love it and ask for the recipe.

Nowadays, you can buy wild rice all year 'round, and much of it comes from California, where it is grown in paddies. I always try, however, to buy the true Minnesota kind.

3 cups water
½ teaspoon salt
¾ tablespoon Hungarian paprika
1 cup wild rice, uncooked
1 medium sweet onion, julienned
8 ounces grape tomatoes
1 (14-ounce) can hearts of palm, coarsely chopped
1 (14-ounce) can artichoke hearts, coarsely chopped
1 red pepper, julienned
1 green pepper, julienned
6 ounces button or baby bella mushrooms,
     uncooked and thinly sliced, optional
fresh basil, optional
4 ounces (or more) feta cheese, crumbled
coarse ground black pepper
1 bottle salad dressing (I prefer a creamy Italian garlic
     from the refrigerated section)

Bring water, salt and paprika to a boil. Add rice, return to a boil. Stir, reduce heat and cover. Cook until rice is tender, about 45 minutes to 1 hour. Remove from heat and cool.

Combine rice with next 7 ingredients and toss thoroughly. Add the cheese and black pepper and mix lightly. Chill salad. Add salad dressing just before serving.

Yield: 6 to 8 servings

Cook's Notes: Rice can be made a day or two ahead. This salad will keep for a couple of days in the refrigerator.

Goulashsuppe

Ruth's German Haus ◆ Goodhue County

2 tablespoons oil	1 (16-ounce) can diced
2 tablespoons butter	tomatoes
2 pounds lean beef chuck,	¼ teaspoon caraway seeds
cut into ¾-inch cubes	1 bay leaf
salt and pepper	4 cups beef broth
2 cups onion, chopped	1 cup water
1 green pepper,	2 medium potatoes,
chopped fine	finely diced
3 garlic cloves, minced	2 carrots, finely diced
2 tablespoons paprika	

Heat butter and oil together in a 5-quart pot. Season beef with salt and pepper, and brown in small batches. Remove and reserve. Reduce heat to low. Add onions, green peppers, and garlic and cook slowly for 15 minutes, stirring occasionally. Add paprika and cook another 2 minutes. Return beef to pot. Add remaining ingredients. Bring to a boil, reduce heat, and simmer for at least 1 hour. Season to taste with salt and pepper.

Yield: 6 to 8 servings

Cook's Note: Goulashsuppe is even better when served the second day, allowing the flavors to fully develop.

Cannelloni

Submitted by Diane Whalen for Ryan ◆ Dodge County

Ryan is a member of Eden Progressive Gophers 4-H Club and was in 6th grade when he participated in the 2007 Favorite Food Show. At this annual event, 4-Hers prepare a recipe, plan a menu around that dish and create a theme with a place setting and centerpiece. The judge asks about their dish, how it was prepared, what the nutritional value is, what the cost per serving is and more.

Pasta:
1 (1-pound) box manicotti pasta noodles

Filling:

2 tablespoon olive oil
¼ cup onion, chopped
1 clove garlic, minced
1 pound ground beef
½ teaspoon oregano
¼ teaspoon salt
pinch of black pepper

1 (10-ounce) package frozen
    chopped spinach
2 tablespoons butter, melted
5 tablespoons cheese, grated
2 tablespoons cream
2 eggs

Tomato Sauce:
3 cups (24-ounce) canned tomato sauce

White Sauce:
6 tablespoons butter
6 tablespoons flour
1 cup whole milk
1 cup cream
pinch of white pepper
¼ teaspoon salt
Parmesan cheese
butter

Pasta: Cook pasta according to package directions. Drain.

Filling: Heat oil in skillet; sauté onion and garlic about 3 minutes. Add ground beef, oregano, salt and pepper and brown. Stir in spinach until dry. Stir in remainder of filling ingredients after removing from heat. Stuff pasta tubes and set aside.

White Sauce: Form a roux by melting the butter in a medium sauce pan. Add flour and stir until smooth. Gradually whisk in whole milk and cream on medium heat while stirring constantly. Stir until thickened to form a sauce. Season with pepper and salt.

Layering and Baking Directions: Grease a 9x13-inch baking pan. Spread 1 cup of tomato sauce on bottom of pan. Place stuffed noodles evenly about the pan for next layer. Pour white sauce over Cannelloni (stuffed pasta containing meat and seasoning). Then layer with remaining 2 cups of tomato sauce. Garnish with Parmesan cheese and butter (cut into pieces) across top. Bake at 350° until warmed through 25 to 35 minutes.

Yield: 6 to 8 servings

Clara's Ham Balls

Clara Graner ◆ Wabasha County

A farmhand favorite, we used this recipe to feed the guys on the farm after a hard day of work. Any leftovers made for great sandwiches the next day in the field.

2½ pounds ground ham	2 cups milk
2 pounds of lean ground pork	3 (10¾-ounce) cans tomato soup
1 pound ground beef	¾ cup vinegar
3 eggs	1½ cups brown sugar
3 cups graham cracker crumbs	2 teaspoons dry mustard

Combine ham, pork, beef, eggs, graham cracker crumbs and milk. Form into 1½-inch balls and place in a shallow pan. In a separate bowl, combine tomato soup, vinegar, brown sugar and dry mustard. Pour over meat balls and bake uncovered for 1 hour at 350°.

Yield: 20 to 24 servings, ¼ pound of meat per serving

Cook's Note: Serve with mashed potatoes, green beans and homemade buns.

Pancit Bihon

Therisa Puerto ◆ Scott County

This is a traditional recipe from the Philippines. It's a favorite party dish to bring to any type of gathering. Think of it as the Philippine version of tater tot hotdish.

2 cloves garlic, minced
1 medium onion, thinly sliced
2 tablespoons cooking oil
2 cups cooked beef, pork, or chicken, diced or cut into stir fry type strips (or a combination of all three to make it extra special)
1 package (7-ounces) small shrimp, uncooked
4 teaspoons oyster sauce
1 teaspoon black pepper
1 teaspoon salt
10 tablespoons soy sauce
1 cup carrots, sliced (julienne strips are best)
2 cups cabbage, shredded
1 cup sweet peas
5 cups beef or chicken stock
1 package (16-ounces) rice stick noodles

Garnish:
green onions
sliced hard boiled eggs
lemon wedges

In a skillet or wok, sauté garlic and onion in oil until golden brown. Add the meat and shrimp. Season the mixture with oyster sauce, pepper, salt and soy sauce. Add vegetables and stock. Bring to a boil until vegetables are crisp-tender. Remove the meat and vegetables from the mixture. Cook noodles in the sauce for 2 to 3 minutes. Remove the cooked noodles from the pan and arrange on a platter. Sprinkle the meat and vegetable mixture over the noodles. Garnish with green onions, boiled eggs, and lemon wedges.

Yield: Fills a large pan

Cook's Note: You could use pre-cooked chicken strips or cubes in this recipe as well as bagged shredded cabbage to shorten the prep time. You can also use any size or shape of rice stick noodles and vary the meat and veggies as you choose.

Rhubarb Chili Cubano

Vicki Torkelson—Scandinavian Inn B & B ◆ Fillmore County

2 tablespoons vegetable oil
½ cup onion, chopped
3 garlic cloves, minced
1 pound ground pork
1 pound ground beef
1 (14½-ounce) can beef broth
1 (28-ounce) can crushed tomatoes
2 tablespoons balsamic vinegar
⅓ cup raisins
2 tablespoons chili powder
½ teaspoon ground allspice
¼ teaspoon ground cloves
½ teaspoon salt
1 (14-ounce) can black beans
1 to 2 cups rhubarb, depending on taste
¼ cup almonds, slivered

Heat vegetable oil in Dutch oven. Stir in the onions and garlic and cook until soft. Add the pork and beef and cook until browned. Drain off the excess fat. Add the beef broth and tomatoes. Stir in the vinegar, raisins, spices and salt. Bring to a boil; reduce the heat and cook for 30 minutes more. Add the black beans, rhubarb and almonds and cook an additional 10 minutes.

Yield: 8 servings

Cook's Notes: If you like, add the rhubarb earlier and cook until it "melts."

Sirloin and Gravy

Carol Anderson ◆ Steele County

My mother was known to everyone as "Little Grandma" — she even received mail addressed to Little Grandma. She wasn't quite five feet tall and weighed around 100 pounds. She loved to cook and did so right up to the end of her life at 98½ years.

Everyone loved her cooking, and that was one of the special things they remembered about her. During the war years my parents had German prisoners from the war camps in Steele County work on the farm, and they thoroughly enjoyed the wonderful meals my mother prepared.

She was known for her homemade buns (with their special ingredient), her homegrown apple pies and her sirloin and gravy. She would check on the apple tree on the farm all summer, watching the progress of the apples for those special pies. She loved to share them with family, friends and neighbors. Her buns were always made for special events, holidays and the family picnic. She would make the dough in a large metal bowl that her mother bought her for her wedding in 1936. I still treasure it.

She loved teaching her three grandchildren how to cook, and many hours were spent with them sharing her love of cooking.

This Sirloin and Gravy recipe was given to her by her mother-in-law in the 1930s. My mother always fixed the meat the night before and got up a little early in the morning because it takes awhile to prepare, but it was worth it! Now we serve it for special occasions and holidays.

Sirloin:
> 2 pounds sirloin steak, cut ½ inch thick
> ½ cup flour
> salt and pepper to taste
> 1 tablespoon lard or shortening
> 2 carrots, diced
> 1 small onion, diced
> salt and pepper to taste

Gravy:
> flour mixture from above
> cold water
> seasonings, if needed

Sirloin: Cut in serving pieces enough for family. Tenderize with meat mallet. Combine flour, salt and pepper; mix well. Roll sirloin pieces in flour mixture (save flour for gravy) and brown in electric frying pan in lard or shortening. Remove from skillet and place meat in roaster. Add carrots and onion to meat. Make gravy and pour over meat and vegetables; cover and simmer for 1 hour at 350° or until meat is tender. Taste for seasoning and add more salt and pepper as needed.

Gravy: Add flour mixture to pan drippings in frying pan; stir until well mixed. Gradually add cold water and mix well again. Keep stirring over medium heat until all lumps disappear. Make enough gravy to cover the meat. May need to add seasonings to make a nice, brown gravy.

Yield: 8 servings

Cook's Note: Serve with mashed potatoes, buttered carrots, fruit salad, homemade pickles, homemade buns, coffee or tea and homemade apple pie.

Creamy Chicken

Betty McKay ◆ Fillmore County

8 chicken breasts
1 (10¾-ounce) can cream of mushroom soup
¼ cup dry white wine
8 slices Swiss cheese
2 cups herb seasoned bread crumbs
2 tablespoons melted butter

Use a 9x13-inch pan. Lay chicken in pan. Mix soup and wine then pour over chicken. Top each piece of chicken with slice of cheese. Cover with crumbs. Drizzle butter over. Bake at 350° for 45 to 60 minutes.

Yield: 8 servings

Depression Era Boiled Dinner

Shirley Laettinger ✦ Wabasha County

This is a wonderful meal that cooked all day on the old green-and-ivory kitchen range, bought from the Sears and Roebuck catalog. It was fired by corn cobs and wood, but later an oil burner was inserted into the fire box, which made it much easier to keep the temperature accurate.

All the vegetables were raised in our garden except the celery. We waxed the parsnips and rutabagas with paraffin for winter use and put the carrots in a huge crock of sand or in a barrel of leaves to preserve them. Potatoes were kept in the basement root cellar.

When electricity came to rural farms, farm women were happy to get an electric stove and refrigerator to make their work easier. Today, many farm wives have jobs in town and need shortcuts to feed their families.

> 1 ham bone from a baked ham or 2 ham hocks
> 3 quarts water
> 6 carrots, cut in 2-inch slices
> 6 parsnips, cut in 2-inch slices
> 1 rutabaga, cut in 1-inch squares
> 2 onions, sliced
> 1 head of cabbage, cut into 8 wedges
> 2 stalks of celery, cut in 2-inch lengths
> 6 medium potatoes, cut in generous hunks
> salt and pepper to taste

Cook the ham bone or hocks slowly for 2 hours in 3 quarts of water in a very large kettle or canner. Then add all vegetables except the potatoes and simmer 2 to 3 hours. Add salt and pepper to taste. Add potatoes the last 40 minutes.

Yield: 4 servings

Aaron's Crispy Chicken Strips

Submitted by Diane Whalen for Aaron ◆ Dodge County

Aaron is a member of Canisteo 4-H Club and was in 4th grade when he participated in the 2007 Favorite Food Show. At this annual event, 4-Hers prepare a recipe, plan a menu around that dish and create a theme with a place setting and centerpiece. The judge asks about their dish, how it was prepared, what the nutritional value is, what the cost per serving is and more.

Aaron loves ranch dressing and is always looking for new ways to include it in foods that he enjoys. He and his mom came up with this recipe.

> 1 (20-ounce) package boneless, skinless chicken breasts,
>   cut into strips
> 1 cup flour
> ¾ cup ranch dressing
> ½ to ¾ cup sour cream
> 1 (12½-ounce) bag onion potato chips, crushed

Coat chicken on both sides in flour. Mix ranch dressing and sour cream; dip floured chicken into this mixture. Cover strips with crushed potato chips. Bake at 350° on a greased cookie sheet until crispy and juices run clear.

Yield: 15 to 18 strips

Southeast Minnesota Meatballs and Gravy (Norwegian Style)

Peggy Hanson ◆ Fillmore County

If Fillmore County had its own license plate, it might say "Land of 1,000 Suppers." Most weeks, somewhere in Fillmore County you could go to an American Legion fish fry, 4-H oyster stew and chili supper, fireman's chicken barbeque, senior class turkey dinner, cattlemen's steak fry or pork producers pork-eque. Not to mention church suppers, which provide us unsurpassed opportunities for serious chowing down – all for a good cause. This doesn't even count all the pancake breakfasts, salad luncheons and ice cream socials.

We are now entering the main church supper season, when communal cooking and eating peaks right along with the colors of the leaves. I just got back from Grace Lutheran in Peterson, where we enjoyed "old-fashioned meatballs". This means they aren't pre-made and frozen in big boxes from a big-box store. They are hand shaped fresh, with a special recipe made by a local grocery. They tasted great.

I am planning to enjoy my 18th consecutive ham and meatball supper at Union Prairie Lutheran Church – always the first Sunday in October. It's one of my favorites, maybe because it was my first Fillmore County church supper. The ham and homegrown squash are excellent, and you can choose from a wide variety of pies, usually including custard, rhubarb, apple, cherry, pecan, pumpkin, blueberry, sour cream raisin, chocolate cream and my favorite, lemon meringue. I salute the pie bakers of Union Prairie – they do good work, and I hope they continue to offer dessert diversity at their supper.

One thing I like about church suppers is their predictability. The menus stay the same year after year. In this fast-changing and uncertain world, isn't it nice to know that Bethlehem Lutheran in Lanesboro will serve you glazed carrots with your meatballs and real mashed potatoes? Can you imagine if they dared switch to rutabagas or something exotic like Brussels sprouts? I'm not sure about this, but changing the vegetable at the meatball supper just might get them in trouble with the bishop – or worse.

Another thing I appreciate about our local church suppers is the care and time that goes into making many things from scratch. I have it on good authority that a dozen men and women labored on a hot day in August to freeze 22 five-quart pails of corn for the Harmony Methodist roast beef supper. Starting about 7 a.m., the men picked and shucked the corn. Then the women silked it, boiled it, cooled it, cut if off the cob and froze it. At noon the workers enjoyed fresh corn on the cob. We are fortunate indeed to live in a place where this kind of food preparation and fellowship still happens on a regular basis. We can do our part to keep these traditions going by showing up at a few church suppers this fall. Maybe you could even volunteer to work at one!

Meatballs:
1 pound ground beef
½ pound ground pork (or another ½ pound ground beef)
1 cup soft bread crumbs
½ cup milk
1 egg, beaten
¼ cup onion, finely chopped
¼ cup parsley, finely chopped
1 teaspoon salt
½ teaspoon each of ginger, allspice, nutmeg and pepper
2 tablespoon oil or butter

Gravy:
2 tablespoons flour
2 cups warm beef broth

Meatballs: Mix all ingredients thoroughly. Form into balls of desired size. In a skillet, sauté in oil or butter until browned. Remove meatballs from pan.

Gravy: Add flour to pan juices and stir over medium heat to mix. After about 5 minutes, add about 2 cups warm beef broth, preferably home-made. Stir with a whisk until smooth. Return meatballs to pan, warm and serve.

Yield: 6 to 8 servings

Chicken and the "Nickel" Noodles

Mark F. Peterson – Minnesota Sesquicentennial Commission member ◆ Winona County

I'll admit I was a fussy eater when I was young. Almost every weekend, we would go from our home to my grandparents' farm nine miles southwest of Mankato near Rapidan Dam in Blue Earth County. My grandparents, Fred and Anna Washburn, bought the farm in 1911 and moved there from near Attica, Ind.

Since I was always reluctant to try new foods, my grandmother paid me a nickel once to try her chicken and noodles. My sister Mary resented the fact I got paid for doing something she had already done for nothing. From that day on, I understood why this was everybody's favorite meal. After my grandmother passed away, my mother continued to make them.

One day my girlfriend (now wife) decided she would impress me by making chicken and noodles. She got the recipe, but had never seen them. I made the huge mistake of saying something like, "These aren't like my mother's," and she swore she would never make them again. I married her anyway, and she stuck to her word.

After many years I gave up and began making them myself for special occasions, and they are now a big part of our family Christmas dinners. We are certain this recipe goes back at least four generations in our family, and I believe it will be made in our family for a long time to come.

Chicken:
1 whole chicken, baked and de-boned

Broth:
pan drippings
chicken flavored soup base
4 to 6 cups water
salt, celery salt and onion salt, to taste
paprika

"Nickel" Noodles:
7 to 14 eggs, depending on number being served
1 to 2 tablespoons butter for every 7 eggs
½ teaspoon salt
¼ teaspoon baking powder
flour

Chicken: Bake chicken in the oven and when done de-bone the meat, cut into chunks and set aside.

Nickel Noodles: Use anywhere from 7 to 14 eggs depending on number being served, noodles are great heated up as leftovers. Put eggs in large bowl and beat. Add about 1 to 2 tablespoons of butter for every 7 eggs, salt and baking powder. Add enough flour until the noodle dough isn't sticky.

Cut up 3 grocery bags and lay flat on table (I tape them together on the bottom) and sprinkle with flour. Roll out the dough to approximately ¼ inch thickness. Let dry for about 2 to 3 hours. Roll dough into a cylinder and then cut to about ¼ inch wide strips and unfurl; let lay to further dry while bringing the broth to a boil.

Broth: Put the drippings from the chicken in a large pot. Add chicken flavored soup base, seasonings to taste and water. Bring to a boil and slowly add noodles and chunked chicken and bring to a full boil. Cook chicken and noodles until done (about 20 minutes). Sprinkle a bit of paprika on top when serving.

Hammed Eggs

Karl Reuter Family ◆ Blue Earth County

This is an old Polish-German recipe that has been passed down through the generations, and it's still enjoyed by the Reuter family today. It wouldn't be Easter without Hammed Eggs! We serve huge bowls of Hammed Eggs (shells on) with ham and our other favorite Easter eggs such as traditional dyed eggs, colored deviled eggs, "jiggler" eggs and homemade chocolate truffle eggs.

> ham (with bone in) or ham bone with some meat still on
> onion, cut into large pieces
> eggs, as many as will fit in pot with ham

Place all ingredients in a large pot. Cover with water. Bring water to a boil, reduce heat and simmer for 4 to 5 hours or more. Eggs will be hard boiled and a pinkish brown color inside. The hammed eggs will peel easily and will also have a subtle ham flavor. The ham will be very tender, fall off the bone, and have a mild flavor.

Yield: Dozens; however many will fit in the pot with the ham

Classic Rosewood's Chicken and Cabbage Panade

Dick and Pam Thorsen ◆ Dakota County

The Queen Anne-style Classic Rosewood is on the National Register of Historic Places, but was built as a home in 1880 by Rudolf and Marie Latto, who came to Minnesota from Bavaria. The Lattos left their home to the City of Hastings for use as a hospital; later it was converted to a nursing home.

We saved it from demolition in 1988, and after doing a certified restoration, opened Classic Rosewood in 1989 with five rooms. Today we have eight. We are different from a bed and breakfast because we also serve dinner (using local and organic produce) but only to our overnight guests. Marie Latto started out as a cook – in what history calls a shack – for the rafters on the river. We have a hard time cooking in Marie's former home without feeling her kindly critique, and we think she would be happy we are serving rafters (travelers) of a different sort today.

3 tablespoons butter	1 loaf French bread
½ head cabbage, shredded	¼ to ½ cup Parmesan
5 to 6 carrots, shredded	cheese, shredded
½ clove garlic, minced	3 tablespoons Swiss cheese,
2 chicken breasts, skinned	shredded
1 quart chicken broth, or a little less	

Melt butter in big kettle. Add cabbage, carrots and garlic. Sauté until partially cooked. At the same time poach chicken breasts. Slice half of the loaf of bread into 1-inch thick slices and toast in the oven on a cookie sheet while the chicken cooks. When chicken is done and not pink in the middle, cut into 1½-inch pieces and add to cabbage mixture.

Place 2 slices of toasted bread in the bottom of a large, oven-safe, tureen. Sprinkle with a little Parmesan cheese and add ½ of the chicken/cabbage mixture. Then layer 2 or 3 more slices of toasted bread 1 layer thick. How many slices will depend on the size of your tureen and the size of your bread. Add the rest of the mixture and more cheese and then top with more toasted bread.

Add broth down the side of the tureen being careful to not get the bread wet with it. Bake in a preheated oven at 350° for 45 minutes. Take out and sprinkle remaining Parmesan and Swiss cheese on top. Bake until it melts nicely and seals the soup under the bread (10 to 15 more minutes). Serve in tureen.

Yield: 6 to 8 servings

Cook's Note: You can also do this in big individual-serving soup bowls by putting 1 piece of toasted bread on bottom of soup bowl, then a layer of chicken/cabbage mixture and another piece of bread and broth. Bake and finish with cheese and bake for a few minutes more. A panade is a sweet or savory soup made with bread and other ingredients.

Ground Spam Sandwich

Ruth A. Olson ◆ Freeborn County

Spam, made by Hormel, is the main ingredient in this filling, and it's known worldwide. My father retired from Hormel, and so did I. This is a family sandwich filling I have eaten since I was a child in the 1940s.

1 can of SPAM®
3 boiled eggs
1 small onion, chopped
2 large dill pickles
1 clove garlic
1 cup of salad dressing or mayonnaise
buns or bread

Grind all ingredients together, folding in the dressing as the last step. Spread filling on buns or slices of bread.

Yield: 25 servings

Cook's Note: Toasting the open-faced sandwich in a toaster oven or under the broiler for a few minutes also tastes pretty darn good. Serve this sandwich with fruit salad, potato chips and a glass of milk or coffee.

Round-up Stew

Gail Griffin ◆ Winona County

Alternative livestock has become a norm in our county, as have other local foods served at our area eateries. I created this recipe, and it won the 2006 National Bison Cook-Off contest.

Each year in early November, our animals' health is evaluated by our veterinarian. Our industry calls it "round-up." It's more like the wild, wild, West – tenfold! Making this recipe on that day is the only thing easy from sun up to sun down.

1 tablespoon olive oil
2½ pounds buffalo arm roast, silver skin removed
½ teaspoon garlic, minced
1 (10-ounce) can tomato bisque soup
1 envelope onion soup mix
1 cup water
pepper to taste
1 (14½-ounce) can stewed tomatoes
dash balsamic vinegar
1 cup carrots, diced or sliced
1 cup celery, diced
2 cups russet potatoes, peeled and cubed

Heat oil in skillet and sear roast on all sides. Place roast in slow cooker on low heat. Sauté garlic in same pan and add to top of roast. Top roast with soup, dry onion soup mix, water, pepper and tomatoes and cook on low for 6 hours. Stir. After 6 hours, add vinegar, carrots, celery and potatoes to the slow cooker and turn to high for 2 hours. When vegetables are tender, break apart the roast and serve up in bowls.

Yield: 4 to 6 servings

Cook's Note: Have had equal success in preparing in a Dutch oven. Recipe multiplies well for a large crowd. Terrific served up with warm, crusty French bread slices for dunking. Add a mixed fruit salad and the meal is nutritiously delicious!

Grandma Jo's Wild Rice and Beef Casserole

Karen England ◆ Goodhue County

My Grandma Jo recently died at the age of 96. She was born and raised in Minnesota and was sharp until the day she died. She was a wonderful friend and a great example of a Scandinavian Minnesotan. We had Wild Rice and Beef Casserole many, many Saturdays and Sundays at Grandma Jo's house when we were growing up.

4 cups water, boiling
1 cup wild rice, uncooked
¾ cup celery, chopped
6 tablespoons onion, chopped
butter
1 pound ground beef
1 (10¾-ounce) can cream of mushroom soup
1 (10¾-ounce) can cream of chicken soup
1 large can of sliced or button mushrooms, drained
¼ teaspoon pepper
¼ teaspoon paprika
¼ teaspoon garlic salt
2 beef bouillon cubes
1 cup water, boiling

In a large kettle, pour 4 cups boiling water over wild rice and let stand for 15 minutes, drain. In a skillet, sauté celery and onion in butter until transparent. Add to wild rice. Brown ground beef. When brown, drain off fat and add to wild rice mixture. Add mushroom and chicken soups and mushrooms. Season to taste with pepper, paprika and garlic salt. Dissolve 2 bouillon cubes in 1 cup boiling water. Pour all into large glass casserole dish and refrigerate overnight. Bake covered for 1½ hours or more at 350°. Add more beef bouillon if it becomes dry while baking.

Yield: 4 to 6 servings

Beef, Black Bean and Sweet Potato Casserole

Amy Nutoni ◆ Houston County

1 pound ground beef	2 medium sweet potatoes, peeled
1 (8-ounce) can tomato sauce	and thinly sliced
1 tablespoon chili powder	½ cup raisins, chopped
1 teaspoon ground cumin	2 plum tomatoes, chopped
½ teaspoon salt	1 can green chilies, diced
1 (15-ounce) can black beans,	1 small onion, chopped
drained	1 cup Cheddar cheese, shredded

Brown the beef in a skillet and drain off grease. Stir in tomato sauce, chili powder, cumin and salt. Spread the beans in an even layer in a 2½-quart greased baking dish. Layer the potatoes over the beans. Sprinkle with the raisins, tomatoes, chilies and onion. Spread the beef mixture over the vegetables. Cover and bake at 350° for 45 minutes. Uncover, top with cheese and bake 15 minutes or until potatoes are done.

Yield 6 to 8 servings

Owatonna Sweet Corn Au Gratin

Corky, Julie, Jenna and James Ebeling ◆ Steele County

Sweet corn has been grown on our family farm for generations. Ebeling sweet corn is known to be some of the best in Steele County! This recipe is submitted in honor of our parents and grandparents, Jim and Carole Ebeling.

6 ears of fresh corn or 1 quart frozen sweet corn, thawed
3 tablespoons butter
1 small onion, finely chopped
1 green pepper, cored, seeded and finely chopped
3 tablespoons flour
2 cups milk
1 cup Cheddar cheese, shredded
2 eggs, well beaten
1 teaspoon sugar

salt and pepper to taste
½ cup bread crumbs

Preheat oven to 350°. Grease a 2-quart casserole. If fresh corn is used, cut corn from cob. In a large frying pan over medium heat, melt butter. Add onion and green pepper and sauté until tender, stir in flour and then add milk. Cook, stirring constantly, until mixture has thickened and is smooth. Remove from heat and add corn, cheese, eggs, sugar, salt and pepper. Pour into casserole and top with bread crumbs. Bake for 45 minutes.

Yield: 6 servings

Zucchini Hot Dish

Yvonne Cory ◆ Faribault County

I plant a garden every spring and always put in zucchini. It's a summer squash that seems to grow overnight in size, and people make many jokes about it. I use zucchini in cooking, but also take some to the farmers market. I make this hotdish in early to late summer – it's a great meal in one dish. I often take it to gatherings, and it always gets good comments.

4 cups zucchini, unpeeled and sliced
¾ cup carrots, shredded
½ cup onions, diced
6 tablespoons butter or margarine
4 cups chicken, cooked and cubed
½ cup sour cream
1 (10¾-ounce) can cream of chicken soup
½ cup Cheddar cheese, shredded
croutons on top

In a skillet, sauté zucchini, carrots and onions in butter. Put all ingredients except cheese and croutons in a lightly greased 9x13-inch baking dish. Sprinkle cheese on top and croutons over the cheese and bake at 325° for 1 hour or until done and croutons are lightly browned.

Yield: 10 to 12 servings

Church Ladies' Dill Pickles

Peter Flick ◆ Winona County

Shortly after we moved to Winona in 1996, we attended a funeral and the luncheon afterwards. I was struck by the quality of the pickles served, so I asked the lovely, elderly church ladies where they got such delicious pickles. They replied, "We made them." I must have looked puzzled because they added, "Should we tell him, Edith?" She nodded, yes. "We add a tablespoon or two of sugar to a jar of store-bought dills, and let it sit in the refrigerator for a day or two," they said.

I have used this wonderful recipe many times, always with the story of the charming church ladies.

> 1 jar purchased dill pickles
> 1 to 2 tablespoons sugar, depending on size of jar

Add 1 to 2 tablespoons of sugar to the jar of pickles. Close lid tightly and gently shake to distribute the sugar. Refrigerator overnight, and use within 1 week.

Apple Pizza

Rosanne Buehler ◆ Houston County

> 1 tube refrigerated crescent rolls
> 1 cup Cheddar cheese, shredded
> 3 apples, chopped
> ¼ cup sugar
> ¼ teaspoon cinnamon
> 2 tablespoons flour
> butter

Pat rolls onto pizza pan. Sprinkle on cheese and apples. Combine sugar, cinnamon and flour. Sprinkle over apples, dot with butter. Bake at 350° for 30 minutes. Eat warm. Delicious!

Yield: 1 (12-inch) pizza

Caramel Pecan Pound Cake

Pat Staloch ✦ Waseca County

In July 2003, I entered my Caramel Pecan Pound Cake in the Festag celebration in Minnesota Lake. This was my first time entering food in the local fair. I received an award of merit and a blue ribbon. Then in August, I entered the cake in the Waseca County Fair and received a sweepstakes purple ribbon and a blue ribbon. So then I decided to try my luck and entered the cake in the Minnesota State Fair. That was an eye-opening experience for me. When I brought my cake to be displayed, there were many, many cakes – more than I ever imagined. I didn't receive a ribbon, but I did score 82 points.

1 cup butter, no substitutes
2¼ cups brown sugar, packed
1 cup sugar
5 eggs
3 teaspoons vanilla
3 cups flour
½ teaspoon baking powder
½ teaspoon salt
1 cup milk
1 cup pecans, finely chopped
confectioner's sugar

In a mixing bowl, cream butter. Gradually beat in sugars until light and fluffy. Add eggs, one at a time, beating well after each. Stir in vanilla. Combine the flour, baking powder and salt; add to the creamed mixture alternately with milk. Beat on low speed just until blended. Fold in pecans. Pour into a greased and floured 10-inch tube pan. Bake in a preheated oven at 325° for 1½ hours or until a toothpick inserted near the center comes out clean. Cool for 10 minutes before removing from pan to a wire rack to cool completely. Dust with confectioner's sugar.

Yield: 12 to 16 servings

Key Lime Pie

Kathy DeNeui ◆ Faribault County

Rarely do working moms take time to bake or make a pie. There's just no time. This recipe is quick, simple and delicious. No one would ever guess how easy it is!

> 1 (9-inch) baked pie shell
> 1 (14-ounce) can sweetened condensed milk
> ½ cup key lime juice
> 1 (8-ounce) container whipped topping

Beat milk and juice until thick and smooth. Fold in the whipped topping. Spoon into pie shell, chill and enjoy!

Yield: 6 to 8 servings

Helen's Favorite Brownies

Helen Haley ◆ Le Sueur County

These are a favorite for card clubs, church dinners and family gatherings.

> ¾ cup flour
> ¼ teaspoon baking soda
> ¾ cup sugar
> ⅓ cup margarine or butter
> 2 tablespoons water
> 1 (12-ounce) bag semi-sweet chocolate chips
> 1 teaspoon vanilla
> 2 eggs
> ½ cup walnuts, chopped

Preheat oven to 325°. Grease a 9-inch square baking pan. In a small bowl, mix flour and soda. In a saucepan, mix sugar, margarine and water. Bring to a boil over medium heat. Once the mixture has boiled, remove from heat. Stir vanilla and 1 cup of chocolate chips into saucepan mixture until chips are melted. Cool 10 minutes. Stir in eggs. Add flour mixture. Add remaining chocolate chips to the batter. Put batter in pan and sprinkle nuts over the top. Bake 30 minutes.

Yield: 16 servings

Oatmeal Cutout Cookies

Sarah Prunty—in memory of Alma Marquardt ◆ Dodge County

We make these cookies for Christmas every year, and sprinkle them with green and red sugar.

1 cup butter, softened
1 cup sugar
1 teaspoon soda
½ cup buttermilk
1 teaspoon salt
1 teaspoon vanilla
2 cups oatmeal
2 cups flour
cinnamon sugar mixture or green or red sugar

Cream the butter and sugar together. Dissolve soda in buttermilk and add to creamed mixture. Add remaining ingredients. Use additional flour as need to roll dough and cut into shapes. Optional: Sprinkle with cinnamon sugar mixture or green or red sugar or before baking. Bake at 350° for 8 to 10 minutes. Remove from baking sheet and let cool.

Yield: 4 to 5 dozen cutouts

Cook's Note: If someone has an egg allergy, these are a nice alternative to other cookies.

|||||||||||||||||||||||||||||||||||||||||||||||||||||||||||||||||||||||||||

Hazel's $10,000 Cheesecake

Margaret Goderstad ◆ Dakota County

This recipe comes from 98-year-old Hazel Jacobsen Theel, one of the founders of the Dakota County Historical Society. She wrote much of the history of the City of Hastings, and was a leader in getting the downtown buildings and many homes placed on the National Register of Historic Places.

Hazel learned early on that if you feed someone well, they will perform. When she needed money for projects around town such as monuments, she would feed prospective donors this wonderful cheesecake. They couldn't resist and before leaving her table, wrote checks for the necessary projects. Food, and especially this cheesecake, will do it every time!

Crust:
> 2 tablespoons brown sugar
> ¾ cup walnuts, finely chopped
> ¾ cup graham crackers, finely crushed
> 3 tablespoons butter, melted

Filling:
> 4 (8-ounce) packages cream cheese, softened
> 4 eggs
> 1½ cups sugar
> 1 tablespoon fresh lemon juice
> 2 teaspoons vanilla

Topping:
> 2 cups sour cream
> ¼ cup sugar
> 1 teaspoon vanilla
>
> fresh or frozen fruit
> whipped cream

Crust: Mix brown sugar, chopped walnuts, graham cracker crumbs and melted butter; pat into a 9- or 10-inch springform pan. Set aside.

Filling: Mix with beater, cream cheese, eggs, sugar, lemon juice and vanilla until well blended. Spread mixture on top of graham cracker mixture. Bake in a preheated oven at 350° for 45 minutes. Remove from oven and let cool for 15 minutes.

Topping: Mix sour cream, sugar and vanilla and put on top of cheesecake. Bake an additional 15 minutes at 350°.

Let cool for several hours and serve with fresh or frozen strawberries, raspberries or other seasonal fruit and a dollop of whipping cream.

Yield: 8 servings

Cook's Note: Freezes very well.

Raisin Cookies

Connie Garmann ◆ Faribault County

1 cup white raisins	2 eggs
1 cup water	2 cups quick cooking oatmeal
½ cup sugar plus 2 teaspoons	2 cups flour, sifted
	½ teaspoon salt
2 teaspoons baking soda	1½ teaspoons cinnamon
½ cup brown sugar, packed	1½ teaspoons vanilla
1 cup shortening	

Cook white raisins and 2 teaspoons sugar in water until tender. Drain off liquid and save 5 tablespoons. Add baking soda to raisin liquid; add mixture to raisins. Cream together ½ cup sugar, brown sugar and shortening. Add eggs, 1 at a time. Blend in oatmeal, flour, salt and cinnamon. Stir in vanilla. Add raisin mixture to butter, mix well. Drop by teaspoons on cookie sheet. Bake in a preheated oven at 375° until brown.

Yield: 4 to 5 dozen cookies

Butterscotch Bars

Jackie Haley ◆ Waseca County

This is a great summertime recipe because it doesn't heat up the house when you make them. The bars are a nice alternative to chocolate.

> ½ cup margarine
> 1 cup peanut butter
> 1 (12-ounce) package butterscotch chips
> 3 cups miniature marshmallows

Melt margarine, peanut butter and butterscotch chips together. Cool slightly and stir in marshmallows. Mix well. Grease 9x13-inch pan. Spread evenly in pan. Keep refrigerated.

Yield: 24 bars

Cook's Note: Chocolate chips can also be used or ½ chocolate and ½ butterscotch chips.

Rhubarb Brunch Cake

Kathy Neutz ◆ Scott County

> 1 package yellow cake mix
> 1 cup water
> ⅓ cup oil
> 3 eggs
> 4 cups rhubarb, sliced
> 1 cup sugar
> 2 cups whipping cream

Combine cake, water, oil and egg. Beat with mixer on low about 1 minute, then on high 2 minutes. Pour into greased 9x13-inch pan. Top with rhubarb, sprinkle with sugar. Pour cream over top. Bake at 350° for 1 hour or until tooth pick inserted at the center comes out clean.

Yield: 16 servings

Marshmallow Cake

Mabel Krautbauer ◆ Waseca County

I have made more than 70 birthday cakes for grandchildren and some great-grand kids, but quit when I was 85 years old. I made butterflies, Mickey and Minnie Mouse, a rocking horse, hot-air balloon, clowns, Snoopy, airplanes and many more.

When I made this cake and took it to church doings, they would say, "Oh, Mabel brought her famous cake!"

Cake:
> 1 ½ cups sugar
> 2 cups cake flour, sifted
> 1 cup boiling water
> 3 teaspoons baking powder
> ¼ teaspoon salt
> ½ teaspoon cream of tartar
> 5 egg whites, room temperature
> 1 teaspoon vanilla

Frosting:
> 2 egg whites, room temperature
> ½ teaspoon cream of tartar
> ⅓ cup sugar
> ⅓ cup corn syrup

Cake: Mix first 3 ingredients, stirring and mixing well, then let stand until cool. Add 3 teaspoons baking powder to the flour/water mixture. Add salt and cream of tartar to the 5 egg whites and beat until they hold shape. Fold flour/water mixture into egg whites and gently mix well. Then add 1 teaspoon vanilla. Grease 9x13-inch pan and dust with flour. Pour mixture into pan and bake in a preheated oven at 350° for 40 minutes. When toothpick is inserted in the center and comes out clean, it's done.

Frosting: Beat egg whites and cream of tartar until they hold shape or make a peak when you lift the beater up. Boil sugar and corn syrup until it spins a thread when you lift the spoon out. Add to the beaten egg whites, beating all the time. Spread on cake.

Yield: 12 to 15 servings

Norwegian Sweet Soup

Orlie C. Grant ◆ Mower County

In 2009, our Norwegian Lutheran church will celebrate its 150th anniversary. I have belonged to this church all my life. Many lutefisk dinners with all the good food trimmings — like this sweet soup — have been served there.

½ (4-ounce) package sago
5 cups cold water
1 pound prunes, pitted
5 cups cold water
¼ teaspoon salt
¼ stick cinnamon
2 tablespoons lemon juice
½ cup sugar
½ cup currants
1 cup golden raisins
1 cup raisins
2 cups water
red food coloring, optional
⅓ cup grape juice or wine

Soak sago in 5 cups water overnight. Simmer for 30 minutes or longer. Stir often. Cook prunes, 5 cups water, salt, cinnamon stick, lemon juice and sugar for about 20 to 30 minutes.

In separate pan, combine currants and raisins and 2 cups water and simmer for 10 minutes. Mix together sago, prunes and raisin mixture and simmer 5 minutes, add a few drops of red food coloring, if desired. Add wine and cool.

Yield: Makes 3 quarts

Cook's Note: Sago is similar to pearl tapioca. You can substitute ¼ cup pearl tapioca for the sago. You can also use 3 tablespoons of quick-cooking tapioca which doesn't require overnight soaking and only needs to be cooked for 10 to 15 minutes.

Pumpkin Ice Cream Dessert

Helen Swendiman ◆ Mower County

Instead of pumpkin pie, this dessert has become a Thanksgiving tradition in our family.

Crust:
  ¾ cup graham cracker crumbs
  ¾ cup gingersnap cookie crumbs
  ¼ cup sugar
  ¼ cup butter

Filling:
  1½ cups pumpkin, canned
  1 cup brown sugar, packed
  1 teaspoon cinnamon
  ¼ teaspoon salt
  ½ teaspoon ginger
  1 quart vanilla ice cream, softened
  whipped cream, optional

Crust: Mix the crust ingredients and press into a 9-inch square pan, reserving ½ cup for top.

Filling: Blend pumpkin, brown sugar, cinnamon, salt and ginger. Add ice cream and fold together. Pour into crust, sprinkle with reserved cookie crumbs. Freeze and serve with whipped cream on top.

Yield: 9 to 12 servings

Snowy Glazed Apple Squares

Rosanne Buehler ◆ Houston County

La Crescent is the apple capital of Minnesota. My husband and I operate Leidel's Apple Stand, Leidel's Apples and Orchard in La Crescent. This is one of my favorite recipes. We make it for many events including the Church of the Crucifixion's annual dinner, the Chamber of Commerce's dinner at the Depot and The Slice of Life 5k Run.

Squares:
2½ cups flour, sifted
½ teaspoon salt
1 cup shortening
2 eggs, separated
milk
1½ cups corn flakes, crushed
8 medium size tart apples, pared and sliced, about 5 cups
1 cup sugar
1½ teaspoons cinnamon

Glaze:
1¼ cups powdered sugar, sifted
3 tablespoons water
½ teaspoon vanilla

Squares: Combine flour and salt in bowl. Cut in shortening. Beat egg yolks and add enough milk to make ⅔ cup. Add to pastry mixture; toss lightly. Divide dough in half. Roll 1 portion to fit a 9x15-inch jelly roll pan. Sprinkle with corn flakes. Spread apples over flakes. Combine sugar and cinnamon; sprinkle over apples. Roll out remaining dough. Place on top, seal edges. Beat egg whites until foamy. Spread on crust. Bake at 350° for 1 hour. Cool slightly. Spread with glaze.

Glaze: Combine powdered sugar, water and vanilla. Spread over slightly cooled squares.

Yield: 15 to 18 servings

SOUTHWEST REGION

In the Southwest, the land opens into cornfields, then grasslands. The Minnesota River angles through the region's terrain and history. Rhubarb for coffee cakes, muffins and pies springs eternal in backyards everywhere.

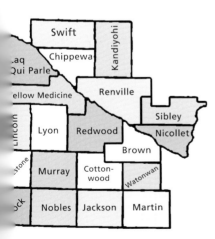

Vegetable gardens and fruit trees produce a bounty that graces the table from summer to fall, then into the winter, preserved in glowing jars of red, orange and green. This is pork and cattle and pheasant country, too. A cornucopia for the region's cooks!

Cappuccino Punch

Colleen McGinty Bents ◆ Nobles County

This refreshing punch is wonderful served for breakfast or brunch, as an afternoon cooler with cookies or biscotti, at a wedding, graduation, reception, party or anytime.

½ cup sugar
¼ cup instant coffee
1 cup water, boiling
2 quarts milk
1 quart vanilla ice cream, softened
1 quart chocolate ice cream, softened

In a small bowl combine the sugar and coffee. Add boiling water and stir until dissolved. Cover and refrigerate until well chilled. Just before serving pour coffee mixture into a gallon pitcher or punch bowl. Stir in milk. Add scoops of ice cream and stir until melted.

Yield: 1 gallon

Cook's Note: This freezes well, if it lasts that long!

Town Party Lemonade

Laura Ingalls Wilder Museum ◆ Redwood County

The Charles Ingalls family lived around and in Walnut Grove from 1874 through 1879. It was a luxury to have lemons in the 1870s in Minnesota. This recipe was made by Mrs. Olson and served at Nellie's town party to Laura and her sister Mary.

"'Is your lemonade sweet enough?' Mrs. Olson asked. So Laura knew that it was lemonade in the glasses. She had never tasted anything like it."

– From *On the Banks of Plum Creek*, written by Laura Ingalls Wilder about her life in Walnut Grove.

⅔ cup sugar
1 cup water
3 large lemons
3 cups cold water
ice

Stir ⅔ cup water with sugar until dissolved. Cut lemons in half and squeeze out juice. Be sure to remove the seeds. Stir sugar water with lemon juice and add cold water. Pour lemonade over ice in glasses.

Yield: 6 glasses

Grandpa's Punch

Stanley H. Bergemann ◆ Watonwan County

I believe this is an original recipe of my own. If you put good things in, then good things come out. I make it for our grandchildren's christenings, birthday parties, graduations and other occasions. Although I have never tried it, if it were an all adult party, maybe you could add a fifth of vodka! Everyone asks me for the recipe, and I tell them – KISS: Keep it Simple, Simon.

1 (64-ounce) bottle cranberry cocktail juice, chilled
1 (12-ounce) can frozen lemonade, chilled and thawed
1 (2-liter) bottle Squirt®, chilled
1 large molded frozen ice chunk, 32- to 40-ounces
1 large punch bowl

Pour cranberry cocktail in punch bowl. Add lemonade concentrate and stir. Slowly add soda, down along the bowl edge and gently stir. Add large ice chunk. Allow guests to serve themselves.

Yield: 20 (4-ounce) servings

Garlic Butter Spread

Tom Zera ◆ Nicollet County

I was at home and hungry for something to eat. It was getting late, so going to a restaurant or the grocery store was out. I decided to look at what I had in the kitchen and found bread, butter, garlic, basil and some other condiments. When I thought about what I could make from those items, it hit me – Garlic Butter Spread. Eureka!

½ pound unsalted butter, softened
1 ½ teaspoons garlic, minced
3 to 4 leaves fresh basil
pinch of black pepper
1 baguette

Preheat oven to 350°.

In a food processor combine butter, garlic, basil and black pepper. Pulse the ingredients until they are fully mixed together. Once all the ingredients are fully combined evenly, let rest.

Take the baguette and cut it open lengthwise. Spread the garlic spread onto the baguette evenly. Place the bread onto a cookie sheet. Bake for about 5 minutes. Check the bread and continue to watch until it begins to get crispy and golden brown on the edges.

Yield: 16 slices

Hot Bean Dip

Mary Crawford ♦ Rock County

1 pound ground beef, browned
1 (16-ounce) can kidney beans, drained and mashed
1 teaspoon chili powder
1 onion, chopped
¾ cup ketchup
1 cup Cheddar cheese, shredded
tortilla chips

Combine beef, kidney beans, chili powder, onion and ketchup. Top with cheese. Put in 1½-quart casserole dish and bake 30 minutes at 300°. Serve with tortilla chips.

Yield: Approximately 3½ cups dip

Lon's Pickled Eggs

Scott Myhre ♦ Lyon County

1½ cups vinegar
2 cups water
4 teaspoons salt
1 teaspoon pickling spice
2 teaspoons sugar
1 clove garlic
1 dozen hard boiled eggs, peeled

Combine in a large glass jar. Refrigerate.

Yield: 12 eggs

Caramel Kick Snack Mix

Denice Evers ◆ Brown County

This snack mix has a spicy kick – yes the amounts for chili powder and ground red pepper are correct! But once people try it, they always request the recipe. It's a great snack for watching TV, a card party or other occasions.

6 cups plain bite-size white corn tortilla chips
5 cups of Crispix® cereal
1 bag microwave popcorn, popped, remove unpopped kernels
1 (12- to 16-ounce) can of mixed nuts or peanuts
½ cup butter
½ cup light corn syrup
¼ scant teaspoon cinnamon
½ cup packed brown sugar
1 tablespoon chili powder
¼ teaspoon ground red pepper

In a large bowl mix tortilla chips, cereal, popcorn and nuts. In a saucepan, bring the butter, light corn syrup, cinnamon, brown sugar, chili powder and red pepper to a boil. Pour this caramel mixture over the cereal mixture and stir until the cereal is coated. Spread out on 1 or 2 cookie sheets and bake at 250° for 1 hour, stirring every 20 minutes.

Yield: 8 to 12 servings

Hoppel Poppel

Bobbi McCrea ◆ Brown County

Hoppel Poppel is a rich, yummy traditional German dish, often served for breakfast and found throughout the old country with regional variations. In the United States, it's primarily a Midwestern dish. Hoppel Poppel doesn't translate; it's just a funny name like "scramble" for an American breakfast medley of eggs, meat and potatoes.

In the rhyme "Pottkieker," the child asks, "Mama, Mama, what's in the pot?" To which Mama impatiently replies, "Hoppel poppel, appel reis, mach'dich fort, Naseweis." (Hoppel poppel, apple rice, now get lost, nosy child.)

> 1 cup sauerkraut, drained
> 6 large potatoes, peeled, boiled and diced
> 6 large pre-cooked sausage links
> 1 carrot, grated
> ½ teaspoon dill or 1 sprig fresh dill
> pepper to taste
> ¼ cup whipping cream
> 3 large eggs
> 1 cup Swiss cheese, grated (or your choice)

Mix sauerkraut and potatoes gently and spread in bottom of greased 9x11-inch pan. Slice sausage links and place over potato mixture. Add carrots, dill, pepper and cream. Beat eggs and add on top. Sprinkle with grated cheese. Bake at 325° for 25 minutes or until set, can then keep on warm somewhat indefinitely.

Yield: 12 servings

Cook's note: This dish is very easily modified, and can even be made without the eggs. I serve this at The Bohemian Bed and Breakfast as a main dish for breakfast, along with beans and pears and maybe a hearty bread.

Company Eggs

Karen Ruehling ◆ Sibley County

S ibley County produces millions of eggs each year.

1 pound breakfast sausage
4 cups croutons
4 eggs, beaten
¾ cup milk
1 teaspoon dry mustard
8 ounces Cheddar cheese, shredded
1 (10¾-ounce) can cream of mushroom soup
1 cup half-and-half

Brown sausage in fry pan. Place croutons in bottom of 13x9-inch pan. Add browned sausage. Mix beaten eggs, milk and dry mustard. Pour over sausage. Mix cheese, soup and half-and-half; pour over sausage and croutons. Refrigerate overnight. Bake 45 minutes at 350°.

Yield: 10 to 12 servings

Cook's note: This dish freezes well.

Big Dee's Hashbrowns

Jodi Lund ◆ Renville County

T hese hashbrowns were created by Deloris Lund and became her signature dish. They were usually served once a month at the Fairfax VFW along with steak on the grill or pork chops, coleslaw, baked beans and fresh warm bread balls...mmm!

10 (1½-pound) bags frozen hashbrowns,
    loose and shredded
5 envelopes onion soup mix, dry
1½ pounds butter, no substitution

Place all ingredients in an electric roaster and heat for approximately 2 to 3 hours at 350°. Stir often. When hashbrowns are heated, turn heat to warm. Enjoy!

Yield: 1 (18-quart) electric roaster

Cook's Notes: Amount of butter can be adjusted up or down depending on your taste.

Sweet Salsa

Rich Sullivan ◆ Redwood County

20 cups tomatoes, chopped
3 cups onions, chopped
7 large yellow banana peppers, chopped
2 green peppers, chopped
8 to 12 jalapeño peppers, chopped
5 garlic cloves, chopped
2 cups sugar
4 tablespoons chili powder
4 tablespoons salt
2½ cups vinegar
2 to 3 tablespoons cornstarch

Mix tomatoes, onions, peppers and garlic; add sugar. Simmer on stove for 20 to 30 minutes, stirring often. In a separate bowl, mix vinegar and cornstarch. Add this to the pepper mixture slowly, it will thicken quickly. Cook another 10 to 15 minutes and pour into hot sterilized pint jars ½-inch from top. Add lids and screw bands to seal. Process jars in a hot water bath for 10 to 15 minutes. Remove and cool on rack or towel on counter.

Yield: 10 pints

Danish Aebleskiver
(or Ebleskiver or Ableskiver)

Valeria Christensen ◆ Lincoln County

My Christensen grandparents emigrated from Denmark. My grandfather, Jens, came in 1901, and then his bride, Valborg, in 1916. With her came the traditions of Danish cooking and baking. When they purchased farmland from the railroad, they chose to settle in southwest Minnesota, close to Tyler, where there was a higher concentration of Danes. Tyler continues to embrace its Danish heritage with an annual festival in the summer called Aebleskiver Days.

Grandma Christensen was widowed at an early age and continued to make her home on the farm with her son, Waldemar, who had five children, including me. When I was a child, watching Grandma cooking Aebleskivers on special occasions was always such a treat because she used a knitting needle to turn them to cause less "disturbance." The delicious pancake pastry was light and fun to eat with the "surprise" in the middle.

Later, as my Mom and siblings continued to prepare Aebleskiver, we used forks and pans that were designed for gas or electric stoves, unlike Grandma's knitting needles and her original Aebleskiver pan for the cook stove.

I've passed on many Danish traditions to my son, John, including the skill of cooking his own Aebleskivers. It's a wonderful tradition and one I'm thrilled to continue.

    3 eggs, separated
    2 tablespoons sugar
    ½ teaspoon salt
    2 cups buttermilk
    2 cups flour
    1 teaspoon baking soda
    1 teaspoon baking powder

Beat egg yolks until light and lemon colored. Add sugar, salt and buttermilk. Mix well. Sift together flour, baking soda and baking powder. Add to egg mixture. Beat egg whites until stiff and fold into batter. Place a small amount of shortening in each cup of an Aebleskiver pan and fill ⅔ full of batter. Cook over medium heat until bubbly, then turn carefully with fork and finish baking on other side. Turn each Aebleskiver several times to ensure thorough baking.

Yield: 2½ dozen

Cook's Notes: The Aebleskiver pan has either 9 or 7 indentations in the skillet that look like small round cups about the size of golf balls. If desired, place a very thin slice of apple or small amount of applesauce into the batter in each cup before turning. We often have Aebleskiver for Christmas Day or Easter breakfast, but always with strong coffee. Serve with butter and syrup, jam, brown sugar or sprinkle lightly with confectioner's sugar.

Specken Dicken

Jeanne Hoidal Cleary ◆ Kandiyohi County

This recipe is an old German recipe from the Klaahsen side of my family. Although I don't make it, many family members carry on the tradition.

> 3 cups rye flour
> 1 cup white flour
> 2 teaspoons baking powder
> 1 teaspoon salt
> 1 cup dark syrup
> ½ cup sugar
> a sprinkle of cinnamon
> milk, if necessary
> bacon, bologna and pork sausage or
> summer sausage, cut into pieces

Mix flours, baking powder, salt, syrup, sugar and cinnamon together; may thin with milk. Place pieces of meat in fry pan, then pour batter over and place more meat on top. Be sure the pan is hot, flip when bubbling.

Coffee Time Basic Scones

Deb Foley ◆ Kandiyohi County

These scones make a great treat for breakfast or morning or afternoon coffee break. I've made them several times for my co-workers, and they all asked for the recipe.

Scones:
 3 cups flour
 ½ cup granulated sugar
 2½ teaspoons baking powder
 1 teaspoon salt
 ½ teaspoon baking soda
 ¾ cup butter, cold, cut into cubes
 1 cup buttermilk, this can be powdered buttermilk made
  according to container
 2 tablespoons heavy cream
 2 teaspoons sugar

Extras:
 ¾ cup chopped apricots, ½ cup chopped pecans,
  2 tablespoons orange zest
 ½ cup dried blueberries, ½ cup white chocolate chips,
  2 tablespoons lemon zest
 1 cup cinnamon chips, ½ cup white chocolate chips,
  1 teaspoon cinnamon
 ¾ cup dried cranberries, ½ cup white chocolate chips,
  2 tablespoons orange zest

Scones: Preheat oven to 425°. In a large bowl, mix together the flour, sugar, baking powder, salt and baking soda. Cut butter into flour mixture with pastry blender until mixture is crumbly. Mix in extras of your choosing. Add the buttermilk and stir until the dough is rough and shaggy.

Gather the dough together and place on a generously floured work surface. Knead gently about 10 times. Divide dough in half and pat each piece into a circle about 7 inches in diameter and ½ inch thick. Brush circles with cream and sprinkle with sugar. Cut each round into

8 pie-shaped wedges. Place the scones, barely touching, on a baking stone. Bake until puffy and golden, about 15 to 18 minutes.

Yield: 16 scone wedges

Cook's Notes: I serve these scones at breakfast with an egg bake and fruit compote.

Whole Wheat Honey Bread

Marcia Hemstad Haley ◆ Chippewa County

Growing up in Chippewa County, this was one of my favorite recipes to make, and it always turns out delicious.

> 2 packages dry yeast
> 1 tablespoon sugar
> 1 cup warm water
> 1 tablespoon salt
> ½ cup honey
> ½ cup cooking oil
> 2 cups water
> 4 cups whole wheat flour
> 4 to 5 cups white flour

In large bowl, combine yeast, sugar and warm water. Stir; let stand 15 minutes. Add salt, honey, oil and water; stir. Add the flours gradually; knead for 10 minutes. Cover; let rise about 2 hours or until double in size. Knead again; divide into 3 loaves. Place in well greased loaf pans; let rise. Bake in a preheated oven at 350° for 25 to 35 minutes.

Yield: 3 loaves

Bread Machine Zwieback

Vicki Rasmussen ◆ Cottonwood County

One of the most popular Mennonite foods in Cottonwood County is zwieback. It may be the only Mennonite food dating back to the time of Menno Simons (1496-1561), the founder of the Mennonite religion. This food is so much a part of the Mennonite heritage that streets in the Netherlands bear its name. Mennonites brought zwieback with them to North and South America. Today it's still popular and Mountain Lake is renowned for its zwieback.

Zwieback are shaped by pinching off a ball from the rich dough and placing it on a pan. A second, smaller ball is pinched off and pressed deeply into the first so it will not topple off while baking. Considerable skill is involved in getting them to stay upright together. Tops that slide off or lean over are "lazy zwieback." A familiar Mennonite saying is, "If one bun is left without a partner, you can expect company after church."

Zwieback baking is part of the Saturday ritual, along with cleaning the house and preparing food for Sunday. A weekend without zwieback is hardly a weekend at all. They are served on Sunday for breakfast and again for afternoon coffee or faspa. If any remain, they are toasted in the oven. When done properly, the toasted buns last indefinitely.

This recipe uses a bread machine, which makes zwieback easier for busy cooks.

> 2 cups skim milk, scalded
> ½ cup oil
> ¼ cup sugar
> 1 ½ teaspoons salt
> 4¾ cups bread flour, sifted
> 2½ teaspoons dry yeast

Scald milk and put in bread machine bucket. Add oil, sugar, salt and flour. Make a hole in the flour and add yeast. Wait 10 minutes for milk to cool down and start bread machine on dough cycle. When bread machine is through mixing and just starts the rise cycle, remove dough from bucket and let rise in a well-greased bowl for 1 hour. Punch down and shape into zwieback.

Shape zwieback by pinching off a ball of dough and placing it on a pan. A second, smaller ball is pinched off and pressed deeply into the first so it will not topple off while baking. Let rise for 1 hour and bake in a preheated oven at 400º for 12 minutes.

Cook's note: For best results, use sifted flour specifically designated for bread machines.

Bea Burns' Indian Fry Bread

Pipestone County Historical Society ◆ Pipestone County

Indian Fry Bread is made for powwows – festive gatherings of Native Americans. Most often it's used in Indian Tacos. Toppings of hamburger, chopped tomatoes, cheese, lettuce, sour cream and onions are piled on top of the bread. Indian Tacos are sold at restaurants in Pipestone and the Indian Center makes them for fundraisers.

Bea Burns' grandmother, who was of the Peoria tribe, named her "The Listener" when she was born. Bea and husband, Bill, came to Pipestone in 1929 as employees of the Pipestone Indian School. She was the boys' housemother at the school until it closed in 1952 and was affectionately known as "Mom Bea" to the hundreds of Native American boys under her care. Bea was a member of the Hiawatha Club and played the role of Nokomis in the Song of Hiawatha Pageant for 32 years. She passed away in 1991 at the age of 93.

4 cups flour	2 tablespoons baking powder
3 tablespoons sugar	2 tablespoons cooking oil
¾ teaspoon salt	1⅔ cups water
⅔ cup powdered milk	

Sift together dry ingredients. Mix with oil and water as for biscuits. Let rest one hour. Pinch off in pieces a little larger than a walnut, flatten, poke hole in center and fry in an electric fry pan at 350° until lightly brown, turn and brown other side.

Yield: 10 servings

Chicken Gumbo Soup

Donna Mae Kock ♦ Watonwan County

½ cup green bell pepper, chopped
1½ cups frozen okra, cut in ½-inch pieces
½ cup onion, chopped
3 tablespoons margarine
2 (14½-ounce) cans chicken broth
1 (1 pound, 12-ounce) can diced tomatoes
1 small bay leaf
½ cup water
1 chicken bouillon cube
salt and pepper to taste
1 tablespoon minced parsley
1 cup rice, cooked
1 cup chicken, cooked and finely diced

Simmer green pepper, okra and onion in margarine until soft. Add broth, tomatoes, bay leaf, water and bouillon cube and simmer gently for 15 minutes. Season with salt and pepper to taste. Add the parsley, rice and chicken. Heat thoroughly and serve.

Yield: 6 servings

Cook's Notes: Serve this gumbo with fresh bread and a green salad on a cold winter evening.

Sweet Potato Slaw

Karen Albrecht ✦ Nicollet County

This salad uses raw sweet potatoes. I misplaced it once and tried to find a similar one on the Internet, but no luck. That's when I found out how unique it is!

Slaw:
> 3 cups raw sweet potatoes, peeled and shredded
> 1 (20-ounce) can pineapple, drained and chopped
> 1 apple, chopped
> ½ cup pecans, chopped

Dressing:
> ½ cup sour cream
> ½ cup salad dressing, light
> 2 tablespoons lemon juice
> lemon zest
> 2 tablespoons honey
> salt and pepper to taste

Slaw: In large bowl, combine potatoes, pineapple, apple and pecans.

Dressing: Mix sour cream, salad dressing, lemon juice, lemon zest, honey, salt and pepper. Stir into salad mixture. Chill before serving for flavors to develop.

Yield: 8 to 12 servings

Cook's Notes: Excellent with grilled salmon or pork tenderloin.

Minnesota Tomatoes

Linda Sullivan ◆ Redwood County

This is a great way to preserve wonderful summer vegetables. I like to keep it on hand as a base for hotdishes and to make dinner for unexpected company.

> 12 cups tomatoes, peeled and quartered
> 1 cup celery, chopped
> ½ cup onion, chopped
> 3 teaspoons salt
> ½ cup green pepper, chopped

Simmer chopped vegetables for 10 minutes. Pour into clean, sterilized (hot) canning jars, filling ½ inch from top. Put on lids and rings and process for 50 minutes in hot water bath in canner. Remove and place on rack to cool and seal jars.

Yield: 10 to 15 pints

Cook's Note: For a quick hotdish on top of the stove, I add hamburger, ketchup and macaroni.

Dairy Frost BBQs

Cindy K. Schweiss ◆ Renville County

For many years Fairfax was lucky enough to have a "mom-and-pop" Dairy Frost, of which I was the proud owner for nine years. Fairfax is a big baseball town, and the Dairy Frost was located just one block from our baseball stadium and swimming pool. BBQs, Coneys and hot dogs were a quick and easy meal before, during or after a baseball game or quick swim.

When I bought the business, the "secret recipe" was part of the deal. Whether served on buns alone or on hot dogs and foot-longs as Coneys, the Dairy Frost BBQs were a Fairfax favorite!

5 pounds lean ground beef	1 cup dried onion
2 (10¾-ounce) cans tomato soup	1 cup water
2 (10- to 12-ounce) bottles chili sauce	30 to 35 buns

Brown and drain ground beef, add remaining ingredients and mix well. Put into a large sealable container. Mixture can be divided in half and frozen. When ready to serve a crowd, thaw mixture and heat in slow cooker for 6 hours or heat on stovetop or in oven. Serve on buns.

Yield: 30 to 35 sandwiches

Cook's note: This sandwich was served with chips, pickles and a soda. It's perfect for a quick meal because it's made ahead and serves a crowd.

French Dip Sandwich with au Jus

Vicki Rasmussen ◆ Cottonwood County

1 (3-pound) beef chuck roast, trimmed
2 cups water
½ cup soy sauce
1 teaspoon dried rosemary
1 teaspoon dried thyme
1 teaspoon garlic powder
1 bay leaf
3 to 4 peppercorns
8 French rolls, split, toasted and buttered

Place roast in a slow cooker. Add water, soy sauce and seasonings. Cover and cook on high for 5 to 6 hours or until beef is tender. Remove meat from broth; shred with forks and keep warm. Strain broth; skim off fat. Pour broth into small cups for dipping. Serve beef on buttered and toasted rolls.

Yield: 8 servings

Grandma Pack's Swiss Steak

Annette DeCourcy Towler ✦ Redwood County

Sunday noon dinner in a parsonage was a challenge when you had to be at two church services. Since that was our big meal of the day, this was the easiest recipe to make and have baking while we were at church. This is an old Pack family recipe we still make today as a special meal when family gets together.

I have called it Swiss Steak Sunday Dinner in the Parsonage. My daughter calls it "How long do you pound it?"

2 pounds round steak	6 large carrots, peeled and
¼ cup flour	sliced
1 teaspoon salt	the long way
½ teaspoon pepper	2 cup onions, sliced
2 tablespoons oil	1 quart tomato juice, or more
6 potatoes, peeled and	1 quart stewed tomatoes
quartered	

Wipe meat with damp cloth; trim off excess fat and cut into serving pieces. Combine flour, salt and pepper and pound into meat with the dull edge of a butcher knife. Heat oil and brown the meat on both sides. Transfer meat and oil to large pan/roaster pan (minimum size 9x13-inches). Put potatoes, carrots and onion on top. Add tomato juice and stewed tomatoes. Moisture needs to cover the meat, so use more tomato juice if needed. On stove, heat the pan until juices are boiling. Remove to the oven and cook at 300° for 4 hours. When done remove potatoes, meat and carrots to a serving plate. You can make gravy from the sauce that is left in the pan. Also sauce in the pan can be served without flour added. Good either way.

Yield: 6 to 8 servings

Cook's Note: This recipe can be done in a slow cooker for 4 to 6 hours. Amounts of potatoes, meat and carrots can be adjusted to family food likes or number of people you are serving. I use half of a large baking potato per person.

Veal Loaf

George L. Glotzbach ◆ Brown County

This recipe represents the German-style cooking popular in New Ulm since the 1860s. It came to me through three generations of my German-Bohemian family. During the 1930s, '40s and '50s, this was a popular, made-to-order meat mixture at Schnobrich's Meat Market on Minnesota Street in New Ulm. It was called, "Glotzbach Veal Loaf."

> 1 pound fresh ground veal (from leg, if available)
> 4 ounces ground salt pork
> 1 egg
> ¾ cup cracker crumbs (reserve about 1 tablespoon
>   for topping)
> 1 tablespoon onion, minced
> 1 tablespoon green peppers, minced
> ½ cup milk
> 1 tablespoon butter
> seasoned salt and pepper to taste

Take ground veal and ground salt pork and mix well in bowl. Mix in egg, cracker crumbs, minced onion and green peppers. Then add enough milk (about ½ cup) to moisten well and form a loaf. Add seasoned salt (sparingly because of salt pork) and pepper to season.

Mix all ingredients with hands to form a loaf. To bake, use a small, buttered loaf pan. Place crumbs on top and dot with butter. Bake at 325° for 1 hour, basting every 20 minutes.

Yield: 1 loaf

Cook's Note: Pan drippings make a fine gravy. Recipe may be doubled or tripled but increase baking time accordingly. For a hearty winter menu, serve glueh wein (a warm, spiced wine), lentil soup, cucumber salad, veal loaf, mashed potatoes with gravy and Christmas cookies.

Mom's Meatloaf

Cathy Strube Buxengard ◆ Nobles County

My parents met in the Army during World War II. My father was a medic and my mother an Army nurse. Dad was a German from Jackson and Mom an Italian from Chicago. They married and lived in Jackson. It's a predominately German town, and Mom had to learn some new ways of cooking. She made a great meatloaf that is still a hit today with our family. Dad always made the goose at Thanksgiving or Christmas. His stuffing was wonderful. I make it with the Thanksgiving turkey every year, and our kids and grandkids love it.

1½ pounds ground beef
¼ cup onion, minced
1⅓ cups bread crumbs
1 teaspoon salt
1 egg
1 teaspoon horseradish
¾ teaspoon dry mustard
½ cup milk
3 tablespoons ketchup, plus extra for top

Mix all ingredients together. Place in 5x7-inch loaf pan. Spread some extra ketchup on top. Bake at 400° for 1 hour.

Yield: 1 meatloaf

Dad's Stuffing

1½ cups water, boiling
½ to ¾ cup butter
½ cup onion, minced
¼ teaspoon pepper
1 teaspoon poultry seasoning
1½ teaspoons salt
2 tablespoons dry mustard
¼ cup celery, chopped
3 quarts bread cubes
2 tablespoons parsley
giblets, cut up small

Combine water, butter, onion and giblets. Simmer 5 minutes. Add remaining ingredients. Mix well and stuff bird.

Mom's Pizza Burgers

Crystal Vixie ♦ Kandiyohi County

This is my favorite recipe, made with good old Spam from Austin. Every year, my mother would make a meal of our choice on our birthday. I always picked the same thing—Mom's homemade pizza burgers. My brother liked them, too, but would pick something different because he knew he'd share my choice of "birthday supper."

1 pound ground beef
1 can of SPAM®, cut in pieces
1 pound Velveeta® cheese, cut in pieces
1 (15-ounce) can tomato sauce
1 tablespoon sage
1 tablespoon oregano
1 teaspoon parsley flakes
¼ teaspoon salt, optional
10 to 12 hamburger buns

Brown ground beef and drain, save some of the liquid. Cut Spam and Velveeta into pieces, then grind. Add Spam and Velveeta to ground beef with tomato sauce and spices. Spread on bun halves and bake in oven at 425° for 12 to15 minutes.

Yield: 5 to 6 servings

Lutefisk

Susan Ebeling Anderson ◆ Watonwan County

Traditionally, Scandinavians made lutefisk by soaking unsalted dried cod in cold water and then in a mixture of potash lye and water. Today you can buy ready-to-cook lutefisk at some supermarkets and meat markets.

> lutefisk
>
> salt

Preheat oven to 400°. Place lutefisk skin side down on a sheet of aluminum foil and season with salt. Wrap foil tightly around the fish and place on a rack in a large pan and bake 20 minutes for each pound of fish. When done, cut corner from foil and drain out excess water. Serve at once.

Cook's Note: Serve with melted butter, white sauce, boiled potatoes and salad.

Bourbon-Marinated Pork Tenderloin

Ron Singsaas ◆ Yellow Medicine County

There are many pork producers in our area, and people enjoy trying new ways of serving pork. I usually prepare this for large gatherings such as family reunions and picnics. It's great on the grill, too.

> **Marinade:**
> ¼ cup pure maple syrup
> ¼ cup molasses
> ¼ cup Kentucky bourbon
> 2 tablespoons chili sauce
> 4 large garlic bulbs, crushed
>
> 7 to 8 pound pork tenderloin

Marinade: To marinate pork loin, combine maple syrup, molasses, bourbon, chili sauce and crushed garlic bulbs. Mix well in glass dish. Rub marinade over entire pork loin. Refrigerate and let marinate for 8 hours.

Take pork loin out of marinade and sear on all sides on hot grill or frying pan. Let cool 10 minutes, then wrap in foil. Place on baking pan and bake at 350° for 2 hours or until internal temperature is 180°. Unwrap pork loin and let meat rest for 10 minutes. Slice and serve hot.

Yield: Approximately 20 slices

Cook's Note: Serve on Kaiser rolls with German potato salad or other salads.

German Skillet Supper

Darlene Timm ♦ Yellow Medicine County

1 tablespoon butter
2 cups sauerkraut
3 tablespoons brown sugar
½ cup instant rice
1 pound ground beef
1 medium onion
1½ to 2 cups canned tomatoes
salt and pepper, to taste

Melt butter in an electric frying pan at 350°. Add sauerkraut. Sprinkle brown sugar over the sauerkraut. Add rice, ground beef, salt and pepper, onion and canned tomatoes. Cover and simmer over low heat for 45 minutes. Do not stir.

Yield: 4 to 6 servings

Sauerkraut and Bread Dumplings

Wendinger Band & Travel ◆ Nicollet County

We love to serve sauerkraut and dumplings for our Wendinger Family Christmas get-together, which continues the tradition of our German ancestors' delicious home-style cooking.

Sauerkraut:
> 2 quarts sauerkraut, drained
> 1 small package of lean pork, cut into tiny pieces
> 2 tablespoons brown sugar
> 1 tablespoon sugar
> 3 or 4 potatoes, grated

Bread Dumplings:
> 1 loaf white bread, crust removed
> 1 cup boiling water
> 2 eggs
> ½ to ¾ cups flour or potato dumpling mix

Sauerkraut: Drain the liquid from sauerkraut and put in a pressure cooker with fresh water until level with the kraut. Add pork, granulated sugar and brown sugar. Put pressure cooker on the stove, put cover on and have steam nozzle in place. When the steam nozzle starts rocking, turn it down until it stops rocking. Let cook about 20 to 30 minutes. Remove from stove and let the pressure release on its own. When pressure is out, open cover, add the grated potatoes and cook slowly without the cover until thick.

Bread Dumplings: Cut bread in squares and lay on counter overnight to dry. The next day, put the bread in a bowl and pour boiling water over it. Cover the bowl with a towel and let stand for 1 hour. Beat eggs and add to the bread. Work the dough with your hands. Add flour or potato dumpling mix. Work all together with wet hands and form the dumplings. Roll the dumplings in flour. Cover and cook in boiling water for 20 minutes. Do not peek! Serve with sauerkraut.

Yield: Serves about 6 people

Tennessee Whiskey Pork Chops

Bruce W. Peters ◆ Martin County

Martin County has the highest pork production in the state, and this is a tasty way to enjoy it.

½ cup Tennessee whiskey
½ cup apple cider
2 tablespoons brown sugar
1 tablespoon Dijon mustard
¼ teaspoon cayenne pepper
½ teaspoon vanilla extract
4 teaspoons cider vinegar
4 pork chops, about 1-inch thick
couple of tablespoons vegetable oil
salt and pepper to taste
1 tablespoon butter

Whisk whiskey, cider, brown sugar, mustard, cayenne, vanilla and 2 teaspoons of the vinegar together. Transfer about ¼ cup to a 1-gallon zippered plastic bag, add pork chops, press air out of bag and seal. Refrigerate for a couple hours.

Remove chops from bag, pat dry, and discard marinade. Heat oil in large cast iron skillet. Season chops with salt and pepper and cook on both sides until ¾ done. Transfer chops to plate and cover with foil.

Add the rest of the whiskey mixture to the skillet and bring to boil. Cook until reduced to a thick glaze. Reduce heat, get the plate with the chops and drain any juices back to skillet. Add remaining two teaspoons vinegar and the butter to skillet. Simmer until thick and sticky. Turn off heat.

Return chops to skillet and let rest until sauce clings to chops, turning occasionally to coat both sides (and chops are done). Transfer chops to serving platter and spoon sauce over top.

Yield: 4 servings

Cottonwood Pie

John R. Andrews ✦ Lyon County

This is a wild game recipe and recognizes the large number of outdoors enthusiasts and hunters in our state. It's a deep-dish shepherd's pie adapted from an 80-year-old recipe published in *Field and Stream* magazine. The juniper berries are a traditional accompaniment to wild game because they complement the stronger flavors of the meat. We serve it at hunting camp and to the family during the holidays.

Meat Layer:

6 pounds venison, cubed	⅔ cup gin
flour for dusting	1 cup cashews
2 cups olive oil	2 teaspoons salt
6 shallots, minced	4 teaspoons pepper
4 medium white onions, sliced	1 pound portabella
8 cups beef stock	mushrooms, sliced

Bouquet Garni:

¼ cup juniper berries	thyme, hefty pinch
3 bay leaves	rosemary, hefty pinch
parsley, hefty pinch	

Vegetable Layer:
  10 carrots, chopped
  10 celery sticks, chopped
  ½ stick butter

Topping:
  18 medium potatoes, sliced
  1½ sticks butter
  4 cups milk
  paprika

Meat Layer: Dust venison cubes with flour. Heat olive oil in two separate Dutch ovens. Fry 3 pounds venison in each of the Dutch ovens until browned. Add half of the remaining ingredients to each pan.

Bouquet Garni: Mix ingredients and place half of the mixture in each of the Dutch ovens with the meat; bring to a boil and simmer for 1 hour.

Vegetable Layer: Sauté carrots and celery in butter until tender. Layer half the carrots and celery on top of meat mix in Dutch ovens.

Topping: Boil potatoes until tender; drain. Mash with ½ stick butter and milk. Divide potatoes in half and spread over vegetable layer in both Dutch ovens. Dot top of potatoes with the remaining stick of butter and sprinkle with paprika. Cover and continue to cook for 30 more minutes.

Yield: Serves 12 happy hunters

Pheasant en Crème

Andrea Ruesch ◆ Jackson County

The Jackson County Pheasants Forever Chapter is one of the oldest in the state. This recipe celebrates that history.

1 quartered pheasant
1 (10¾-ounce) can cream of chicken soup
½ cup apple juice
4 teaspoons Worcestershire sauce
¾ teaspoon garlic salt
1 (4-ounce) can mushrooms, drained
dash of paprika

Preheat oven to 350°. Place pheasant in an ungreased 9-inch square pan. Mix soup, apple juice, Worcestershire sauce, garlic salt and mushrooms together in a bowl. Pour over pheasant and sprinkle with paprika. Bake uncovered 1½ to 2 hours and baste occasionally.

Rhubarb Jam

Lorraine Halbersma ◆ Pipestone County

This rhubarb jam recipe was passed down from my mother, Martha VandeVoorde. I started making it as a little girl and still make the jam today. It's a favorite of the entire family. Rhubarb grows in almost everyone's backyard, both in town and rural areas of Pipestone County.

> 4 cups of rhubarb, diced
> 4 cups of sugar
> 1½ cups fresh strawberries, cut or
> 1 (10-ounce) package frozen strawberries
> 1 (6-ounce) package strawberry gelatin

Combine rhubarb, sugar and strawberries in saucepan. Boil for 15 minutes, stirring occasionally. Remove from heat and add the strawberry gelatin. Stir well. Pour into heated pint jars and seal or use melted paraffin wax. If using jar lids process jars in boiling water for 5 minutes.

Yield: 2 pints

Chocolate Zucchini Cake

Mary Hames ◆ Brown County

People are always looking for ways to use zucchini, and this is definitely my favorite. My mom gave me this recipe. She and I agree — the more chocolate chips on top, the better!

> ½ cup sugar
> 1 cup brown sugar
> ½ cup butter
> ½ cup vegetable oil
> 3 eggs, beaten
> ½ cup buttermilk
> 1 teaspoon vanilla
> 2½ cups flour
>
> 2 teaspoons baking soda
> ¼ cup cocoa
> ½ teaspoon cinnamon
> ¼ teaspoon allspice
> 2 cups zucchini, peeled
> and grated
> chocolate chips, optional

Cream the sugars, butter and oil. Add beaten eggs, buttermilk and vanilla. Sift dry ingredients together and add to batter, then mix. Stir zucchini into batter. Pour into a greased 9x13-inch pan. Sprinkle top with chocolate chips, if desired. Bake in a preheated oven at 375° for 45 minutes.

Yield: 16 to 20 servings

Banana Cake

Tammy Picht ◆ Lac Qui Parle County

Cake:
  1 yellow cake mix
  1 cup water
  1 teaspoon baking soda
  dash of salt
  2 eggs
  3 bananas, mashed

Frosting:
  1 (5.1-ounce) box instant vanilla pudding
  1 cup milk
  1 (8-ounce) container whipped topping

Cake: Mix all ingredients together well. Pour into greased and floured 9x13-inch pan. Bake in a preheated oven at 350° for 30 to 35 minutes. Cool and frost.

Frosting: Mix pudding mix and milk together until thick. Gently mix in whipped topping. Frost cake; keep refrigerated.

Yield: 18 to 20 servings

Mom's Spice Cake

Carol Siverhus ◆ Chippewa County

During threshing time at our home, it was cook, cook, cook for days. Bake cookies, pies and cakes for the neighborhood threshing crew that would come and stay for as many days as needed. We had a wood cookstove, so wood boxes had to be full, along with some corn cobs to keep the heat just right for baking. And always it was hot outside, besides being hot inside!

Mom would always make many things, but her spice cake was the best. It smelled so good, and the crew ate it all up. I was the "lunch girl" and would go out to the field where the threshing machine was. I'd sit by the grain truck to keep the flies and dogs out of the lunch until the men had eaten their forenoon and afternoon lunches.

Then they would come to the house for dinner. We set the tables two times. There would be meatloaf, roast beef or pork and chicken. Each lady made different things. Mom made meatloaf, mashed potatoes, gravy, green beans, cabbage slaw, pickles, beet pickles, milk and water. Coffee, and lemon pie were served.

The ladies worked very hard, but they must have felt good about it. I know I did and looked forward to threshing time.

Cake:
- ¾ cup soft shortening
- 1¼ cups brown sugar, packed
- 1 cup white sugar
- 3 eggs, beaten thoroughly
- 2¾ cups flour
- 1½ teaspoons soda
- 1½ teaspoons cinnamon
- ¾ teaspoon nutmeg
- ¾ teaspoon cloves
- 1 teaspoon salt
- 1½ cups buttermilk

Brown Sugar Frosting:
- 1 cup brown sugar, packed
- 12 tablespoons cream or half-and-half
- 4 tablespoons butter
- 1 teaspoon vanilla

Cake: Preheat oven to 350°. Cream together the sugars and shortening until fluffy. Beat in the eggs. Sift the dry ingredients together and stir in alternately with the buttermilk. Pour into a greased and floured 9x13-inch oblong pan. Bake for 35 to 40 minutes or until wooden pick inserted in center comes out clean. Cool.

Brown Sugar Frosting: Combine brown sugar and cream. Boil for exactly 3 minutes. Remove from heat and add butter and vanilla. Beat mixture until no longer glossy. If mixture gets too stiff, add a little cream.

Yield: 18 to 20 servings

Basic Cookie Dough

Mary Crawford ◆ Rock County

1 cup shortening
1 cup sugar
1 cup brown sugar, packed
2 eggs
2 cups oatmeal
1 ½ teaspoons baking soda
½ teaspoon salt
1 teaspoon vanilla
2 cups flour
1 to 2 cups of your choice — chocolate chips,
    gumdrops, nuts or raisins

Mix ingredients in order given. Add your choice of chocolate chips, gumdrops, nuts or raisins. Place on cookie sheet and flatten with a sugared glass or just make them as drop cookies. Bake in a preheated oven at 350° degrees for 8 to 10 minutes.

Yield: 3½ dozen cookies

Three Milks Cake (Pastel de Tres Leches)

Yessica Quezada ◆ Renville County

My husband loves this cake, so it's what I make for his birthday. I also like to bake it for the holidays. I believe it represents the different cultures that are now a part of Minnesota. They keep some of their own traditions and recipes while embracing new ones.

Cake:

1½ cups flour
1 teaspoon baking powder
½ teaspoon baking soda
½ cup unsalted butter
1 cup sugar
5 eggs
1 teaspoon vanilla extract

1 can (14-ounce) sweetened condensed milk
1 can (12-ounce) evaporated milk
1 can (8-ounce) [Media crema Nestle] (may substitute 8-ounces half-and-half)

Topping:

1 (8-ounce) tub whipped topping
4 ounces cream cheese
fresh strawberries

Cake: Preheat oven to 350°. Grease and flour a 9x13-inch baking pan. In a medium bowl sift flour, baking powder and baking soda together and set aside. In a large bowl, cream butter and sugar until fluffy. Add eggs and vanilla. Beat well. Add the flour mixture to the butter mixture a little at a time until well blended. Pour batter into pan and bake for 30 minutes. When cake is done, pierce entire top with fork to ensure the milk mixture will soak in. Let it cool.

When cake is cooled combine the sweetened condensed milk, evaporated milk and Media crema Nestle or half-and-half. Pour mixture on cake and refrigerate at least 2 hours.

Topping: Mix the cream cheese and whipped topping together until creamy and smooth. Spread over top of refrigerated cake and garnish with strawberries or your favorite fruit. Store cake in refrigerator.

Yield: 12 to 15 servings

Cook's Note: The cake should be refrigerated until ready to serve. Adjust the milk mixture to your own taste. I like to make two cakes and pour half of the milk mixture onto each cake. However when I am making this for my husband, he likes all of the milk in one cake. I cut the strawberries in half before placing them on the cake.

Charlie Brown Cookies

Tesha Snyder ◆ Yellow Medicine County

This is a very soft cookie that satisfies the chocolate cravings most of us have. I usually freeze pumpkin from my garden and use it in this recipe.

1 cup pumpkin, cooked or canned	1 teaspoon cinnamon
1 cup sugar	½ teaspoon salt
½ cup oil	1 tablespoon milk
1 egg, beaten	1 teaspoon baking soda
2 cups flour	1 teaspoon vanilla
2 teaspoons baking powder	1 cup chocolate chips

Preheat oven to 375°. Mix pumpkin, sugar, oil and egg. Sift flour, baking powder, cinnamon and salt together and add to pumpkin mix. In separate container, dissolve baking soda in milk, then add to cookie dough. Finally, add vanilla and chocolate chips. Bake for 10 to 12 minutes.

Yield: 48 cookies

Bread Pudding

Paula Freeman ◆ Murray County

My mother made bread pudding to use up the dried ends of the homemade bread she made for our family. This recipe is very similar to my mother's. I'm the owner of the Left Bank Café in Slayton and originally submitted this recipe for the Plum Creek Library System's cookbook project.

8 large eggs	1 large loaf stale bread,
¼ cup flour	crusts removed
4 cups half-and-half	raisins, optional
1 ½ cups maple syrup	slices of apple, optional
1 teaspoon vanilla	½ cup pecans, toasted and
dash salt	chopped, optional
dash cinnamon	maple syrup or caramel sauce,
dash nutmeg	optional

Preheat oven to 350°. Butter and flour a 9x13-inch pan. In a large bowl beat eggs lightly. Add the flour and continue to beat until smooth. Add the half-and-half, maple syrup, vanilla, salt, cinnamon and nutmeg and beat the custard well. Using a serrated knife, remove the crust from the bread and cut it into 4x2-inch rectangles. (If the bread is not stale, place the slices in a 200° oven for about 15 minutes until dried, but not toasted.)

Layer half of the bread lengthwise in the pan, overlapping the rows. Ladle half of the custard over the bread evenly until it is soaked.

Optional step: Soak the raisins in hot water to soften them and put a layer of raisins and apples on top of the soaked bread.

Layer rest of the bread and pour rest of the custard over that until it is soaked. Press bread down, if necessary. Sprinkle the pecans on top and cover the pan with foil. Put a dish of water in the bottom of the oven and bake the bread pudding, covered, for about 60 minutes. Remove the foil and bake another 20 minutes or until the top is golden brown. A knife inserted in the middle should come out clean.

Cook's Note: You can serve this with maple syrup or caramel sauce trickled over the top. Both are wonderful, especially served warm.

Ostkaka

Maureen Holmberg ◆ Kandiyohi County

For us Swedes, one of our traditional foods is Ostkaka, a custard-like side dish served cold with a typical Swedish meal. One of the main ingredients is whey. Traditionally, you would cook hot whole milk, then bring out the whey with a rennet tablet, which was time-consuming. It's equally tasty made with cottage cheese and takes about one-fourth the time to prepare.

> 1 cup sugar
> 2 cups heavy cream
> 1 (16-ounce) container large-curd cottage cheese
> 3 eggs, beaten very well
> 1 teaspoon almond extract

Mix in order given. Bake in 2-quart glass dish for 1½ plus hours at 350°. Let cool. Refrigerate.

Yield: 8 to 10 servings

Norwegian Rice Dessert

Greg Nelson Family ◆ Lac Qui Parle County

This is a great dessert to serve on a cold night and tastes just as great warmed up or chilled the next day. It's been a hit as our kids have grown up.

> | | |
> |---|---|
> | 1 cup rice | 1 teaspoon flour |
> | ½ gallon whole milk | 1 egg |
> | 1 cup whipping cream | raisins, optional |
> | 1 cup sugar | sugar and cinnamon |
> | 1 teaspoon salt | |

Simmer rice and milk for 1 hour. Whip together the cream, sugar, salt, flour and egg. Stir into rice/milk mixture. Simmer 15 minutes. Add raisins and sprinkle sugar and cinnamon on top. Serve warm or cold.

Yield: 4 to 6 servings

Rhubarb Pie

Margaret Finnegan ◆ Jackson County

This is a favorite recipe from my mother-in-law Anna (Mathias) Finnegan. Anna's father and mother, John and Elizabeth (Jentgen) Mathias, homesteaded 80 acres in Southbrook Township in Cottonwood County in 1877. They later moved to LaCrosse Township in Jackson County. John and his seven sons were very successful farmers. Anna was the only daughter. Her father left her 400 acres and a nice building site when he died in 1929.

She married John Finnegan in 1927, and had one child – my husband. In the spring after the snow has melted, one of the first green growth to be seen is the rhubarb. Anna would watch it closely. As soon as it was a couple inches high, she would make this rhubarb pie.

Pie Crust:
> 1 cup shortening or lard
> 2 cups flour
> ½ cup water
> pinch of salt

Filling:
> 3 cups rhubarb, finely cut
> 2 cups sugar
> 2 tablespoons flour
> 3 tablespoons cream
> 2 eggs
> pinch of salt

Crust: Mix shortening or lard and flour until crumbly. Add water, form a ball and divide ball in half. Roll out for top and bottom crust. Place one crust in pie pan.

Filling: Place rhubarb in unbaked pie shell. Beat sugar, flour, cream, eggs and salt together. Pour over rhubarb. Cover with top crust. Bake in a preheated oven at 375° for about 1 hour.

Yield: 6 to 8 servings

Cream Cookies (Big White Cookies)

Eldrene Ebert ◆ Sibley County

This recipe has been in our family for 100 years and still is a favorite. Family members are thrilled to get a batch of them for their birthday gifts. They're "Grandma's Treats," and grandchildren love to dip them in milk as an after-school snack.

1¾ cups sugar
2 eggs
½ cup butter, melted
1 cup whipping cream
1 teaspoon vanilla
1 teaspoon soda
4 to 4½ cups flour (enough to make a stiff dough)

Beat the sugar and eggs until light. Add the cooled melted butter, cream and vanilla. Mix the soda with 3 cups of the flour and add to the mixture. Then add enough remaining flour until dough is stiff. Chill dough ½ hour.

Roll dough out on floured surface to ¼-inch thickness. If dough is sticky, roll in more flour. Cut out cookies with 4-inch cutter. Place on greased sheet. Bake at 375° for 11 to 12 minutes. Cool on wire rack.

Yield: 35 cookies

Cook's Note: You may use whipping cream that has turned sour if you like sour cream cookies.

Orange Cookies

Rebecca LeTendre ◆ Murray County

This is my mother's recipe and my favorite cookie. It uses orange zest to give the cookies a delicious, tangy taste. I love making them, and when I take that first bite, I'm instantly drawn back to the kitchen of my childhood and my mom's freshly baked orange cookies. You can't stop at just one of these, so don't even try!

Cookies:
1 ½ cups brown sugar, packed
1 cup shortening
1 cup sour or sweet milk
2 eggs
3 ¼ cups flour
1 teaspoon salt
1 teaspoon vanilla
1 teaspoon baking soda
2 teaspoons baking powder
2 tablespoons orange zest

Orange Icing:
2 cups powdered sugar
¼ to ½ cup butter or shortening
1 tablespoon orange zest
¼ to ½ cup orange juice

Cookies: Cream together sugar, shortening and milk. Add eggs and vanilla. Stir in dry ingredients, mixing well. Drop by teaspoons onto baking sheet. Bake in preheated oven at 350° for 10 to 12 minutes.

Orange Frosting: Combine powdered sugar, butter or shortening and orange zest. Add enough orange juice to make it of spreading consistency.

Yield: Approximately 6 dozen

Hospital Steamed Pudding

Dr. T. G. Birkey ◆ Chippewa County

Long ago in the old hospital, the cooks would prepare this dessert in December for the medical staff's Tuesday evening meeting. It was something to look forward to and remember afterward! It tastes much like the ancient English plum pudding or suet pudding, but no fat is used in it. The sauce can kill you – although it's a nice way to go.

Pudding:
    1½ cups flour
    ¼ cup molasses
    ¼ cup light corn syrup
    ⅓ cup hot water
    2 teaspoons soda
    ½ teaspoon salt
    2 cups wild plums, stones removed

Sauce:
    ½ cup butter
    ½ cup sweet cream
    1 cup sugar
    1 tablespoon flour
    1 teaspoon vanilla

Pudding: Mix all ingredients together. Steam 1½ hours in a greased and floured pan.

Sauce: Mix butter, cream, sugar and flour and cook in a double boiler until thick. Add vanilla when cooked. Serve hot over hot pudding.

Cook's Note: The original recipe called for cranberries, but I've changed it to wild plums.

Swedish Baked Rice

Verna Pillatzki ◆ Swift County

Rice:

1 cup rice	1 tablespoon cornstarch
2 cups water	1 cup sugar
1 teaspoon salt	1 teaspoon almond
5 eggs, separated	extract

Meringue:

5 egg whites	10 tablespoons sugar

Rice: Cook rice in water and salt until done. Blanch and drain. Mix rice and beaten eggs yolks. Add cornstarch, sugar and almond extract. Place in a 9x13-inch cake pan.

Meringue: Beat egg whites and sugar until they mound slightly. Cover rice mixture with meringue. Place cake pan in 350° oven until meringue is brown.

Yield: 8 to 10 servings

Sour Cream Raisin Pie

Bev Wagner ◆ Nobles County

1 (8- or 9-inch) pie shell, baked	1 teaspoon ground cloves
	4 egg yolks
2 cups raisins	2 cups sour cream
2 cups water	2 tablespoons flour
1⅓ cups sugar	whipped cream
1 teaspoon cinnamon	

Combine raisins and water in a heavy saucepan. Bring to boil. Drain and combine raisins with sugar, cinnamon, cloves, egg yolks, sour cream and flour. Cook over medium heat until thick. Pour into a baked pie crust and let cool. Serve with whipped cream.

Yield: 6 to 8 servings

Apple Fish

Lorraine Theobald ◆ Martin County

This is an old family recipe from Germany. The dough originally was formed in the shape of a fish and filled with the apple mixture — hence the name.

Pastry:
> 2 cups sifted flour
> 2 teaspoons baking powder
> ½ teaspoon salt
> 1 cup cream

Filling:
> 3 to 4 cups apples, sliced
> 1 ½ cups sugar
> dash of cinnamon
> 4 eggs
> 1 cup milk

Pastry: Mix all ingredients; makes a very soft dough. Roll out half of the dough as for a pie and place in bottom of 9x13-inch cake pan. Add filling and cover with rest of dough.

Filling: Slice a thick layer of apples into the pan. Add sugar and a little cinnamon over the apples. Beat eggs, add milk and pour mixture over the apples. Cover with rolled out dough.

Bake in a preheated oven at 400° until apples and custard are done, about 45 to 60 minutes.

Yield: 15 to 20 servings

Apple Crisp

Lois Gahler ◆ Watonwan County

4 cups apples, sliced
sugar and cinnamon
½ cup brown sugar
1 cup oatmeal
½ cup flour
¾ teaspoon cinnamon
⅓ cup soft butter or margarine

Line 9x9-inch glass pan with apples. Sprinkle with sugar and cinnamon. Mix the brown sugar, oatmeal, flour, cinnamon and butter or margarine together and sprinkle on top of apples. Bake in a preheated oven at 350° for 40 minutes.

Apricot Snowballs

Myrnetta E. Knudson ◆ Kandiyohi County

24 dried apricots
1 cup flaked coconut
2 teaspoon orange juice
powdered sugar

Chop apricots, put in blender with coconut and orange juice; blend. Form into ¾-inch balls and roll lightly in powdered sugar.

Applesauce Bars with Cream Cheese Frosting

Judy Dorn ◆ Brown County

We have lots of apples in the fall and this recipe goes well with any menu or alone as a snack.

Cake:
- ½ cup white sugar
- ½ cup brown sugar
- ½ cup shortening
- 2 eggs, beaten
- 2 cups flour
- 1 teaspoon cinnamon or 2 teaspoons pumpkin pie spice
- 2 teaspoons soda
- ½ teaspoon salt
- 2 cups applesauce
- ½ teaspoon vanilla
- ½ cup walnuts, chopped
- 1 cup raisins, optional

Frosting:
- 3 ounces cream cheese, softened
- 6 tablespoons butter or margarine, softened
- 1 teaspoon vanilla
- 1¾ cups powdered sugar

Cake: Cream the sugars and shortening together; beat in eggs. Mix flour, cinnamon (or pumpkin pie spice), soda and salt. Add to creamed mixture alternating with applesauce. Add vanilla; stir in walnuts and raisins. Spread in a greased 10x15-inch pan and bake in a preheated oven at 350° for 25 to 30 minutes. Let cool and frost.

Frosting: Mix cream cheese, butter and vanilla until smooth; add powdered sugar and beat until creamy.

Index

Appetizers
Baked Spinach Artichoke Dip 83
Carmel Kick Snack Mix 174
Cheesy Wild Rice Nibblers 3
Farmer's Market Pineapple Salsa 82
Fat Rascals (Potato Cheese Puffs) 3
Fruit Salsa and Cinnamon Chips 2
Garlic Butter Spread 172
Green Chili Dip 128
Honey Dip for Veggies 128
Hot Bean Dip 173
Oriental Chicken Wings 82
Soft Herbed Cheese Spread 43
Sweet Salsa 177

Beverages
Cappuccino Punch 170
Grandpa's Punch 171
Rhubarb Slush 2
Somalian Tea 11
Town Party Lemonade 170
Wassail 42

Breads - Quick
Apple Streusel Muffins 46
Bannock 71
Bea Burns' Indian Fry Bread 183
Blueberry Muffins 47
Bran Muffins 4
Coconut Bread 130
Coffee Time Basic Scones 180
English Muffins 136
Grandma Godfrey's Gingerbread 119
Lefse 5
Marmalade Bread 133
Milch Brote (Milk Bread) 50
Pork and Bean Bread 50
Prize-Winning Streusel Blueberry Coffee Cake 76

Pumpkin Pecan Loaves 6
Rhubarb Sunflower Bread 8
Swedish Toast 4
Yogurt Muffins 49

Breads - Yeast
Blue Ribbon Cream Cheese Coffee Cake 132
Bread Machine Zwieback 182
Clovia Pizza Dough 135
Debby's Shredded Wheat Buns 53
Grandma's Cinnamon Rolls 48
Houska 131
Mother's Povatica 134
This Stuff Should Win a Prize! 52
Whole Wheat Honey Bread 181
Wild Rice Three Grain Bread 54

Breakfast/Brunch
Baked Swedish Pancake 84
Berry Good Breakfast Bake 86
Big Dee's Hashbrowns176
Breakfast Burritos 44
Caramelized French Toast 45
Company Eggs 176
Danish Aebleskiver 178
Hoppel Poppel 175
Maple Pecan French Toast 7
No-Crust Vegetarian Quiche 15
Omelet in a Baggie 42
Specken Dicken 179
Spinach Walnut Feta Quiche 129
Swedish Pancakes 84

Cakes/Cupcakes
Banana Cake 199
Boiled Raisin Cupcakes 27
Butterscotch Nut Torte 29
Caramel Pecan Pound Cake 159
Chocolate Zucchini Cake 198
Coon Rapids Carrot Cake 118
Marshmallow Cake 165
Mom's Spice Cake 200

Rhubarb Brunch Cake 164
Scandinavian Almond Cake 28
Three Milks Cake 202

Cookies/Bars
Basic Cookie Dough 201
Butterscotch Bars 164
Charlie Brown Cookies 203
Chocolate Cherry Bars 30
Chocolate Malted Milk Cookies 120
Cranberry Oatmeal Cookies 121
Cream Cookies (Big White Cookies) 207
Dark Icebox Cookies 30
Easy Sugar Cookies 74
Ginger Creams 31
Grandma Who Who's Strawberry Cookies 122
Helen's Favorite Brownies 160
Krumb Kaka 33
My Most-Requested Sugar Cookies 32
Oatmeal Cutout Cookies 161
Orange Cookies 208
PBM Chocolate Chip Cookies 124
Pfefferneusse 77
Raisin Cookies 163
Rommegrot Bars 35
Rosettes 34
Sandbakkelse 36
Scotch Toffee 74

Desserts
Apple Crisp 212
Apple Fish 211
Apple Pizza 158
Applesauce Bars with Cream Cheese Frosting 213
Apricot Snowballs 212
Bread Pudding 204
Glorified Rhubarb Rice 37
Hazel's $10,000 Cheesecake 162
Hospital Steamed Pudding 209
Ice Cream Sandwich Dessert 79
Mother's Rhubarb Crisp 73
My Sister's Easy Easy Fudge 73

Norwegian Rice Dessert 205
Norwegian Sweet Soup 166
Ostkaka 205
Peanut Cups 123
Pumpkin Ice Cream Dessert 167
Rhubarb Crunch 38
Snowy Glazed Apple Squares 168
Swedish Baked Rice 210
Swedish Kringla 125
Tin Can Ice Cream 39

Entrée - Beef
Barbecued Meatballs 14
Cannelloni 140
Dairy Frost BBQs 186
French Dip Sandwich with au Jus 187
Grandma Pack's Swiss Steak 188
Iron Miner's Pasties 58
Mom's Meatloaf 190
Mom's Pizza Burgers 191
Nasi Goreng a la Nita 60
Pancit Bihon 142
Sirloin and Gravy 144
Southeast Minnesota Meatballs and Gravy 148
Trini's Albondigas 98
Yelena's Famous Russian Beef Stroganoff 62
Ziggy Burgers 18

Entrée - Fish/Seafood
Baked Northern 57
Fish Tacos 10
Greek Shrimp 100
Lutefisk 192
Pickled Fish 101
Shrimp on Sugar Cane 102

Entrée - Miscellaneous
Ground Spam Sandwich 153
Reuben Pizza 99

Entrée - Pork/Veal
Apple Sauerkraut County Pork 67
Bourbon-Marinated Pork Tenderloin 192
Clara's Ham Balls 141
Depression Era Boiled Dinner 146
French Meat Pie (Tourtiere) 16
Pierogies 64
Pork Chops a l'Orange 96
Sauerkraut and Bread Dumplings 194
Sauerkraut Pie 96
Tennessee Whiskey Pork Chops 195
Veal Loaf 189

Entrée - Poultry
Aaron's Crispy Chicken Strips 147
Chicken and the 'Nickel' Noodles 150
Chicken in Thai Green Curry 105
Classic Rosewood's Chicken and Cabbage Panade 152
Creamy Chicken145
Dijon-Grilled Chicken Breasts 103
Russian Kulebiaka 104
Very Hot Chicken 109

Entrée - Vegetarian
Croppas 66
Sharp Cheddar Fondue 106
Veggie Burgers 107

Entrée - Wild Game
Cottonwood Pie 196
Grilled Bison Tenderloin with Lingonberries 108
Joe Lembcke's Slow Cooker Goose 23
Northern Minnesota Venison Meatballs 70
Pheasant en Crème 197
Pheasant in a Crock 110
Rabbit Stew with Dumplings 68
Round-up Stew 154

Hotdish/Casserole
Beef, Black Bean and Sweet Potato Casserole 156
Cabbage Casserole 19
Calico Beans 111

Chicken Crescent Roll Hotdish 21
German Skillet Supper 193
Grandma Jo's Wild Rice and Beef Casserole 155
Hamburger, Wild Rice and Sauerkraut Hotdish 113
Itasca Jambalaya 114
Kielbasa Sausage Hotdish 23
Minnesota Dinner 22
Smoker Baked Beans 59
Traverse County 4-H Chili 25
Wild Rice Chicken Hotdish 115
Wild Rice Hotdish 69
Wild Rice Pheasant Casserole 26
Zucchini Hot Dish 157

Miscellaneous
Church Ladies' Dill Pickles 158
Dad's Stuffing 190
Hammed Eggs 151
Doris Rubenstein's Infamous State Fair Reject Kosher Dill Pickles 117
Lon's Pickled Eggs 173
Overnight Wild Rice 18
Rhubarb Jam 198

Pies
Braham Pie Day Crust 126
Good and Easy Creamed Apple Pie 80
Key Lime Pie 160
Momma Margie's Rhubarb Custard Pie 78
Muskadee Special Pie 40
No-Bake Raspberry-Blackberry Pie 79
Pear Pie 34
Rhubarb Pie 206
Sour Cream Raisin Pie 210
Zucchini Pie 80

Salads
Baked German Potato Salad 91
Chicken Salad in Cheddar Pastry Cups 92
Dandelion Greens 83
Delicious Salad with Poppy Seed Dressing 95
Marge McClaren's Potato Salad 56
Mexican Cabbage Salad 12

Sweet Potato Slaw 185
Wild Rice Salad 138

Soups/Stews/Chilies
Bouja 85
Cheddar Chowder 55
Cheesy Wild Rice Soup 56
Chicken Dumpling Soup 87
Chicken Chili 112
Chicken Gumbo Soup 184
County Clare's Irish Root Soup 94
Creamy Ham and Asparagus Soup 13
Firehouse Potato Soup 137
The Gausman/Janecek Traditional Christmas Eve Oyster Stew 88
Goulaschsuppe 139
Hard Time Soup 9
Hungarian Pottage Soup 51
Jankee Chili 24
Ol' Ranger Chili 72
Pho Beef Soup 90
Pork Chop Stew 116
Pork Hock Soup 88
Rhubarb Chili Cubano 143
Walleye Chowder 70
Wild Rice Soup 12

Vegetables
Grandmother's Homemade Sauerkraut 97
Hungarian Cabbage 99
Kevin's Grilled Veggie Bundles 20
Latin-Spiced Butternut Squash 93
Minnesota Tomatoes 186
Owatonna Sweet Corn Au Gratin 156
Potato Klub (Potato Dumplings) 17

ndex of Contributors

brecht, Karen 185
cott, Joanna 24
nberg, Emily 134
nderson, Carol 144
nderson, J. E. 128
nderson, Shirley 136
nderson, Susan 192
ndrews, John R. 196
d Godfrey House 119
ndt, Betty 79
hman, Maureen 120
uchenpaugh, Faye 9
dovinac, Jean 42
rduson, Rachel 28
rrett, Beverly 124
nson, Patty 30
nts, Colleen 170
rg, Brook 43
rgemann, Stanley 171
key, Dr. T. G. 209
nstihl, Betty 52
yle, MaryJo 106
andt, Betty 76
ouwer, Cherry 80
ehler, Rosanne 158
ehler, Rosanne 168
gge, Caryl J. 33
xengard, Cathy 190
xengard, Cathy 190
hoon, Adrienne 78
rrigan, Marilyn 131
rroll, Cathy 82
ristensen, Valeria 178
ary, Jeanne Hoidal 179
mmonplace Restaurant 107
rbid, Pat 15
ry, Yvonne 157
unty Belles 12
vington, Karen 96
wan, Barb 44

Crawford, Mary 173
Crawford, Mary 201
Danger, Jana 138
DeNeui, Kathy 160
Dorn, Judy 213
Dorow, Brenda 55
Durkee, Lisa 129
Ebeling Family 156
Ebelings 70
Ebert, Eldrene 207
Edlund, Pat 95
Ellingson, Janice 27
England, Karen 155
Erickson, Phyllis 35
Erickson, Shirley 88
Evers, Denice 174
Favreau-Dickie, Kay 73
Finnegan, Margaret 206
Flick, Peter 158
Foley, Deb 180
Foster, Neva 34
Freeman, Paula 204
Gahler, Lois 212
Garmann, Connie 163
Gates, Patti Lee 94
Gebremedhin, Tela A. 109
German, Nicole 99
Geroy, Muriel 5
Glad, Joyce 14
Glander, Kally 29
Glotzbach, George L. 189
Goderstad, Margaret 162
Gonsorowski, Karen 2
Graner, Clara 141
Grant, Orlie C. 166
Griffin, Gail 154
Gunderson, Shirley 38
Halbersma, Lorraine 198
Haley, Helen 160
Haley, Jackie 164

Haley, Marcia Hemstad 181
Halverson, Brian 3
Hames, Mary 198
Hancock Homemakers 13
Hanson, Anne 2
Hanson, Anne 25
Hanson, Anne 37
Hanson, Peggy 148
Happy Hearts 23
Harris, Pam G. 114
Hasbargen, Leanna 56
Hesse, Norma M. 69
Hinneberg, Twyla 4
Hoang, Van-Anh 90
Hoeft, Kathy 128
Holmberg, Maureen 205
Hoof, Larry and Jeanette 91
Hoppe, Andy 79
Houglum, Linda 30
Hugill, Elaine 115
Janecek, Sarah 88
Jensen, Carol 54
Johnson, Sara 83
Karels, Ron 72
Karpman, Sem 104
Kellerman, Debra 70
King, Maria 116
Kinnunen, Faythe 48
Kinnunen, Faythe 74
Knudson, Myrnetta E. 212
Kock, Donna Mae 184
Krautbauer, Mabel 165
Kreger, Deborah 121
Krueger, Mikki 112
Labs, Sonne 8
LaDuke, Judith B. 22
Laettinger, Shirley 146
Lake County Historical
    Society 45, 499
Lardy, Donna V. 123

Larson, Lori 87
Lauer, Anne 103
Lauer, Greg 100
Laura Ingalls Wilder
    Museum 170
Learmont, Nita 60
Leonard, Ramona 137
LeTendre, Rebecca 208
Loeffler, Diane 86
Lovold, Janine 26
Lueth, Vern 77
Lund, Jodi 176
Mach, Wassana 105
Machmeier, Joretta 111
Madsen, Ann and Richard 74
McCrea, Bobbi 175
McGriff, Marilyn 126
McKay, Betty 145
Metz, Peggy 21
Meyer, Ann 66
Meyer, Brenda 50
Miller, Patricia 92
Mustang Steak House 51, 59
Myhre, Scott 173
Nasstrom, Don 34
Nelson Family 205
Nelson, Jan 40
Neutz, Kathy 164
Nguyen, Mai 102
Nutoni, Amy 156
Ojakangas, Beatrice 58
Old Mill State Park 4
Olson, Ruth A. 153
Paul, Rosalie 80
Paulson, Rose 84
Pawlenty, Mary 84
Peil, Kathy 68
Pelican Rapids High
    School 10-12
Pena, Conrad and Christine
98
Peters, Bruce W. 195

Peterson, Mark F. 150
Pettil, Helene 3
Picht, Tammy 199
Pillatzki, Verna 210
Pipestone County
    Historical Society 183
Porter, Maryann 113
Price, Lynnette 39
Prunty, Sarah 161
Puerto, Therisa 142
Quaintance, Verna 56
Quezada, Yessica 202
Quistad, Yelena 62
Raddatz, Mary and
    Marty 46, 67
Rapacz, Diane 36
Rasmussen, Vicki 182, 187
Reuter Family 151
Robinson, Alice 99
Rubenstein, Doris 117
Ruehling, Karen 176
Ruesch, Andrea 197
Ruth's German Haus 139
Saker, Lilly 40
Schaedler, Lois 18
Schafer, Donna 85
Schafer, Jill 19
Schaller, Barb 132
Schey, Deb 53
Schlueter, Chris 110
Schmidt, Isabelle 83
Schmidt, Richard 57
Schwebach, Renee 32
Schweiss, Cindy K. 186
Scruggs, Susan 135
Seeger, Carol 6
Seeger, Carol 16
Serbus, Joan 23
Sessoms, Ann 93
Shelsta, Norman A. 18
Singsaas, Ron 192
Siverhus, Carol 200

Sletten, Heather 73
Smith, Teresa 130
Snyder, Tesha 203
Staloch, Pat 159
Steele, Nancy 133
Sullivan, Linda 186
Sullivan, Rich 177
Swanson, Bob 71
Swanson, Patricia R. 20
Swendiman, Helen 167
Swenson, Kurt J.R. 96
Taggart, Carol Hugill 31
Theobald, Lorraine 211
Thorlacius, Ethel 17
Thorsen, Dick and Pam 152
Timm, Darlene 193
Torkelson, Vicki 143
Towler, Annette 188
Troiber, Laura 118
Tweten, Suzanne 7
Vixie, Crystal 191
Wagner, Bev 210
Wallin, John 47
Weidenborner, Julie 122
Weinzierl, Norma 50
Welch, Shirley 101
Wendinger Band &
    Travel 194
Wennberg, Alex 82
Wennberg, Brent 108
Whalen, Diane 140
Whalen, Diane 147
Wiczek, Marlene 64
Wilde, Amy Swedish 125
Wolters 70
Yancey, Brenda 42
Zera, Tom Garlic 172